Leading
for the
Long Term

**European Real Estate Executives
on Leadership and Management**

WILLIAM J. FERGUSON

With a Foreword by Jeremy H.M. Newsum

**Urban Land
Institute**

About the Urban Land Institute

The Urban Land Institute is a nonprofit research and education organization whose mission is to provide leadership in the responsible use of land and in creating and sustaining thriving communities worldwide.

The Institute maintains a membership representing a broad spectrum of interests and sponsors a wide variety of educational programs and forums to encourage an open exchange of ideas and sharing of experience. ULI initiates research that anticipates emerging land use trends and issues, provides advisory services, and publishes a wide variety of materials to disseminate information on land use development.

Established in 1936, the Institute today has more than 32,000 members and associates from some 92 countries, representing the entire spectrum of the land use and development disciplines. Professionals represented include developers, builders, property owners, investors, architects, public officials, planners, real estate brokers, appraisers, attorneys, engineers, financiers, academics, students, and librarians.

ULI relies heavily on the experience of its members. It is through member involvement and information resources that ULI has been able to set standards of excellence in development practice. The Institute is recognized internationally as one of America's most respected and widely quoted sources of objective information on urban planning, growth, and development.

Urban Land Institute
1025 Thomas Jefferson Street, NW
Suite 500 West
Washington, DC 20007

ULI Europe
29 Gloucester Place
London W1U 8HX
United Kingdom

Library of Congress Cataloging-in-Publication Data

Ferguson, William J.
  Leading for the long term : European real estate executives on leadership and management / William J. Ferguson ; with a foreword by Jeremy Newsum.
    pages cm
  Includes bibliographical references and index.
  ISBN 978-0-87420-295-3 (alk. paper)
  1. Real estate business--Europe--Management. 2. Executives--Europe--Interviews. I. Title.
  HD583.F47 2014
  658.4'092--dc23
                          2014027178

About the Author

William J. Ferguson is chairman and CEO of Ferguson Partners Ltd. and cochairman and co-CEO of FPL Advisory Group. He conducts senior management recruiting assignments, with a specialization in president/chief executive officer searches and recruiting assignments for boards of trustees and boards of directors. He also conducts CEO succession planning assignments and facilitates public company board assessments and senior management assessments.

Before founding Ferguson Partners, Ferguson was a managing director in the Chicago office of Russell Reynolds Associates for ten years, one of the leading international executive recruiting consultants. There, he comanaged the firm's national real estate practice, handling assignments in 11 segments of the commercial and residential real estate industry. Before focusing on real estate, he worked in strategic marketing for General Mills in Minneapolis.

Ferguson has explored what it takes to be a successful business leader and has written several other books on the topic: *Keepers of the Castle: Real Estate Executives on Leadership and Management,* published by the Urban Land Institute in 2009; *Market Discipline—The Competitive Advantage: Lessons for Canada's Real Estate Leaders* (Real Property Association of Canada, 2012); and *The Wisdom of Titans: Secrets of Success from Entrepreneurs Who Rose to the Top* (Bibliomotion, 2013). He holds a BA from Harvard University, where he was a member of Phi Beta Kappa, and an MBA in marketing from the Wharton Graduate School of Business.

Project Staff

Dean Schwanke
Senior Vice President

Adrienne Schmitz
Project Director/Editor

James A. Mulligan
Senior Editor/Manuscript Editor

David James Rose
Associate Editor

Betsy Van Buskirk
Creative Director/Book Designer

Craig Chapman
Director, Publishing Operations

Foreword

BUILDINGS CAN BE ART; they can be collected as trophies or investments; and they might represent valuable endowment or a future pension.
Whatever we ascribe as a building's role, in every case a building is part
of a place. What are cities, after all, but a collection of buildings? To be a
leader in real estate, therefore, one must look beyond the mundane details
of individual buildings—the design, layout, tenants, rent, and so forth—and
consider how a building and its use affects a larger place.

Buildings exist within the context of a city and its culture, history,
and economy, as well as a response to the inspiration of the owners and
the views of politicians and planners. These elements must all figure in
the question of where, when, what, and whether to build. What is more,
these considerations apply equally to large, multiphased developments and
smaller, single assets. All must be evaluated on the basis of the contribution
that use of the building makes to a place.

The real estate industry has often been shortsighted in this regard.
Most recently, in the early years of this century, the industry allowed the
financial engineers to take over. Now, the pendulum has swung back to the
bricks-and-mortar reality of real estate. Who better than real estate professionals to engage, visibly and vocally, in the debate about the development
and revitalization of cities? This is timely in Europe, where we can finally

look forward to a period of new activity following the 2008–2009 crash and the long economic recession that followed. Our cities will once more be the focus of much development. The decade ahead should be exciting, but our industry and its leaders must look beyond immediate opportunities and consider the broader aspects of each building and development.

Of course, the capital-intensive business of real estate must generate a return. Any development on the drawing board needs to be evaluated on the basis of the efficient use of capital and a proper return for the risks undertaken. But here as well, longer-term considerations are important. Undertaking a project that did not meet these criteria would be foolhardy and the result doomed to become a monument to short-term folly.

I am sure that great leaders in this industry have always thought beyond themselves and their own interests. They are accountable for their decisions not only to direct stakeholders, but also to the community and society in general. Embracing this perspective, and the accountability it implies, is the epitome of the long-term view.

In this book, author William J. Ferguson describes the long-term view as a virtue, one that is difficult to put into action because of the constant pressure for the highest short-term returns—which may well come at the expense of long-term performance. The fact is, real estate is inherently long term. Those who fail to fully grasp the implications of this straightforward and oft-repeated maxim will eventually trip up. Sadly, this industry is heavily prone to groupthink and likely to compound flawed approaches, as we can now see happened a decade ago. We became sheep that unthinkingly followed each other into overbuilding and overbuying, paying too much and employing excess leverage.

If we cannot stop being followers, at least let's make sure there are good leaders, people who are in it for the long term: leaders who embrace their responsibility as corporate citizens, who develop properties for the right reasons—beyond profits alone—and ensure that buildings enhance, enliven, and elevate a place.

In this book, you will read about many leaders who over long careers in real estate have distinguished themselves (and here I must exclude myself, honored as I am to be included in the book). Although their stories and experiences are unique, many of these leaders share beliefs and approaches to real estate and leadership, as summarized here by the author.

As CEO of Ferguson Partners Ltd., a well-regarded, global executive recruitment and management consultancy, Bill knows our industry well. And, as he notes in his preface, leadership is his passion and lifelong interest. Here, Bill has put that passion into practice, to see beyond the real estate industry as a snapshot of its current cycle. He, too, has taken a long-term view with the understanding that leadership neither happens in the moment nor is the result of good timing in a favorable environment. Leadership is honed through multiple cycles, including the downturns and crashes when one's mettle is tested and the wisdom or folly of previous investment decisions is exposed.

There is much collective wisdom in this book, gained from decades of experiences both good and bad. The lessons shared in these pages will be invaluable to those who wish to follow in this industry, provided that they, too, embrace the reality that what happens in real estate is imprinted on communities, neighborhoods, and cities for many years—even multiple decades or longer.

To be a leader in real estate is to develop far more than properties. It is to shape and influence people and their places. In the final analysis, buildings are about the people who work, shop, or play in them, and where they call home.

Jeremy H.M. Newsum
Executive Trustee, Grosvenor Estate
Former Chief Executive, the Grosvenor Group Ltd.

Leadership Matters

THROUGHOUT MY 30-PLUS-YEAR CAREER, I have been a student of leadership and have closely studied the notable few leaders who have risen above the rest. My interest has led me in recent years to undertake a global study to identify the attributes of extraordinary leaders and the personal and professional influences that contribute to their success. This book is the latest result in my ongoing quest.

In these pages, distinguished European real estate leaders and executives share their thoughts and perspectives on the industry, as well as on enduring leadership values. As with executives in North America whom I have had the privilege to interview in recent years, these European leaders shared both personal and professional stories. They gave an insider's view of what it takes to succeed in real estate—arguably the most highly cyclical of any industry. In sharing their experiences and lessons learned, these leaders have left an invaluable legacy for those who follow.

Real estate is a global industry. In fact, having a global perspective is a valued trait among real estate executives, particularly those in Europe who have purposefully amassed a variety of international experiences through their educational backgrounds and career paths. Yet against the global backdrop, there are regional flavors—cultural and language

differences, nuances of doing business, and political and regulatory structures. Even the real estate executive with the most global perspective has
at least a bit of a national character or flair from the place he or she calls
home. Thus, leadership truly does think globally while acting locally.

To capture all these factors and influences, I have written four books
so far, each focused on broad leadership themes while also diving deeply
into specific regions and sectors. My first book, *Keepers of the Castle: Real
Estate Executives on Leadership and Management* (Urban Land Institute,
2009), chronicled the transformation of America's largest industry—real
estate—and identified the attributes of CEOs and other leaders who have
guided their businesses through profound growth, from entrepreneurship
to institutionalization. To a person, successful U.S. real estate executives
spoke candidly about the importance of enduring values and culture,
which must be defined, embraced, and emulated at the top. As Lynn C.
Thurber, retired chairman of LaSalle Investment Management, commented in *Keepers*, "My role is to establish the corporate culture, starting
with the way I conduct myself. I make decisions after I listen to input from
a variety of sources. What I've learned about leadership is that integrity is
critically important, and successful firms put their clients first."[1]

Next, my study took me to Canada where, by being principled and
staying the course within that country's tightly knit real estate sector, leaders helped their companies avoid much of the fallout of the 2008 global
economic crisis. As I wrote in that book, *Market Discipline—The Competitive Advantage: Lessons from Canada's Real Estate Leaders* (Real Property
Association of Canada, 2012), whereas the U.S. and European real estate
industries suffered during and immediately after the crisis, the Canadian
industry was largely unscathed and enjoyed an enviably strong position.
Much of the foundation of Canada's leadership success is strict risk management. As Lorne Braithwaite, former president and CEO of Cambridge
Shopping Centres Limited, observed, "I take risks, but I take risks after
phenomenal preparation, and I'm calculating odds all of the time."[2]

My leadership journey inspired me next to study a special group of entrepreneurs—those who built substantial enterprises. For my third book, *The Wisdom of Titans: Secrets of Success from Entrepreneurs Who Rose to the Top* (Bibliomotion, 2013), I interviewed business builders and leaders across multiple service platforms, from real estate to restaurants and entertainment to engineering, to identify what it takes to outpace even other highly successful entrepreneurs to earn "titan" status in building institutional platforms. Specific qualities and traits—some inborn and some developed over a career—that contribute to success in building a human capital–intensive business include pride tempered by humility, along with the generosity to share with others from experience and lessons learned. The secrets of personal success include a passion for the business. As J.W. "Bill" Marriott Jr., executive chairman of Marriott International, observed, "If you can't have fun doing what you're doing, you'd better find something that you enjoy doing because you won't be successful unless you do."[3]

In this, my latest leadership research, I engaged in one-on-one discussions with some of the best-known and most respected leaders in European real estate. These executives shared their views on how they and their organizations survived the most recent downturn—one of the most severe ever. They spoke with candor of lessons learned during and after the financial crisis, yet with the optimism and confidence that comes from having weathered previous storms. They emphasized enduring skills such as maintaining a long-term view, balancing opportunity with risk, and managing businesses across cultures. Chapters 2 through 9 each end with a section titled "Building Blocks of Leadership" highlighting the main points from the interviews.

As you will read, the most successful of senior European real estate executives share three important traits: they are instinctual, they have an appreciation for culture and complexity, and they manage for the long term.

I sincerely thank those who are profiled in these pages for their wisdom and candor: Serge Fautré, Patrick Kanters, Anne Kavanagh, Nicholas Leslau, Jeremy Newsum, Roger Orf, Alexander Otto, Luis José Pereda,

Olivier Piani, Sir John Ritblat, Francis Salway, Pierre Vaquier, and Jon Zehner. Without the gracious participation of each individual, this book would not have been possible.

I would also like to thank Dean Schwanke and Adrienne Schmitz of the Urban Land Institute for their enthusiasm for publishing this book, as well as Serena Althaus, who runs the European real estate business for Ferguson Partners.

Also on the Ferguson Partners team, I would like to thank Kim Chantelois, Beth Shandling, and Julia Gier for their hard work and other editorial endeavors, as well as Patricia Crisafulli, our manuscript consultant.

In this and all my undertakings, I am blessed to have as a partner my wife, Andrea Redmond Ferguson, who allowed me to make time to write and edit this manuscript. As an author herself, she truly appreciates the time required for such a considerable undertaking.

My hope is that all who read these pages will be inspired in their own leadership journeys. Never forget: even in a deal business, leadership matters enormously!

William J. Ferguson

Notes

1. William J. Ferguson, *Keepers of the Castle: Real Estate Executives on Leadership and Management.* (Washington, DC: Urban Land Institute, 2009), 209.

2. William J. Ferguson, *Market Discipline—The Competitive Advantage: Lessons from Canada's Real Estate Leaders.* (Toronto: Real Property Association of Canada [RealPac], 2012), 47.

3. William J. Ferguson, *The Wisdom of Titans: Secrets of Success from Entrepreneurs Who Rose to the Top.* (Brookline, MA: Bibliomotion, 2013), 8.

Contents

blank

CHAPTER ONE

The Lay of the Land

IN ANY BUSINESS OR INDUSTRY, and especially one as cyclical as real estate, the test of a leader comes not when things are going well—when it seems to the uninitiated that the sky's the limit and there's fast money to be made. The real badge of honor is earned over the long haul by persevering through the inevitable downturns. Recognizing that the good times will not last forever and pullbacks are a reality, industry survivors manage businesses prudently by managing risk proactively.

When a downturn becomes more than the typical correction, escalating to crash and crisis, survival is not guaranteed. Only the most prepared, disciplined, and well-capitalized businesses will sustain themselves through the fall. In such times, humility more than hubris dictates survival.

Most of the real estate leaders interviewed for this book admit to surprise at the severity of the 2008–2009 global economic crisis. Even those who had an inkling that a downturn was coming did not expect it to lead to the worst drop in commercial property values since the 1920s.

Although not without their share of scars and lingering bruises, the most notable leaders in European real estate are still standing largely because of their leadership principles. And chief among those principles: avoid the temptation to chase short-term returns in what is, by nature, a long-term business. While overleveraged and overexposed competitors fell by the wayside during the crisis and in its aftermath, companies led by people with long-term strategies were able to stay the course through the downturn and position themselves to seize the first opportunities that emerged. Theirs were the first cranes back on the skyline and the first sizable developments in markets that once again were showing promise.

Yes, timing plays a role in success in the real estate field, as it does in any business or sector. But values matter even more in a transaction-oriented business like real estate. This author's previous book, *Keepers of the Castle*, contains interviews with U.S. real estate executives who endured many cycles, including the most recent fiscal crisis, demonstrating that they understood the fundamentals and never chased the fads as they built great companies with long-term vision. Similarly, in its follow-up, *Market Discipline—The Competitive Advantage: Lessons from Canada's Real Estate Leaders*, a clear connection is made between the value system of Canadian real estate executives and the health of the sector in that country. In Canada, more stringent bank lending practices, strong relationships among real estate leaders in a tightly knit industry, and a general aversion to too much risk exposure shielded the industry from much of the impact of the financial crisis.

In this book, the focus is on Europe, where Ferguson Partners has been active for many years, including at its London office, established in the mid-1990s. Through its executive recruitment activities, the firm has had a front-row view of trends in the industry and an opportunity to observe and relate to its leaders. From this perspective and through the interviews conducted for this book, certain fundamental leadership principles have emerged—such as having the right instincts and experiences, managing risk, and taking the long-term view—that are as central in Europe as they are elsewhere. Other leadership values, however, appear to be more uniquely European, such as stewardship and legacy. There is a real sense of caring for what has been entrusted to the current generation by those who have gone before, as well as a feeling of obligation to provide for those who will follow. In a landscape of such historic depth, the long-term view takes on another dimension.

Other values evidenced among European real estate leaders relate to the reality of running a pan-European business. Even with economic unification of the European Union, significant differences remain among countries in language, culture, and ways of doing business. To bridge these differences, pan-European real estate firms place great value on the local team. This team is crucial to risk management, which becomes even more important in running a pan-European business. Investing in various regions in the United States (West Coast versus East Coast) or in Canada (Toronto versus Vancouver) is not as risky as dealing with the pronounced differences one encounters in Europe. Consider, for example, how different Greece is from Germany—economically, politically, and culturally. The complexities of executing a pan-European strategy are not for the inexperienced.

As the profiles of leaders in the following chapters show, many tend to specialize in a particular market (London, for example) or sector (such as retail). Although their company portfolios may be diverse, their core businesses tend to be focused on those few things they do extremely well. Trying to be all things in all markets carries huge risk, especially during downturns.

The European Environment

The most challenging environment for real estate companies was the global financial and economic meltdown of 2008–2009, which began in the U.S. housing market, detonated in the financial sector, and resulted in decimated investor portfolios. The crisis hit like a tidal wave, buffeting financial and government institutions and ultimately all businesses with unprecedented force. As the European Investment Fund wrote in its 2009 annual report, "2009 was the year in which the global economy experienced its most severe downturn since the Second World War. The unprecedented period from 2008 through 2009 will be recalled as the Great

Recession."[1] To shore up the system, massive government and central bank interventions were launched to avoid doomsday scenarios. Across Europe, plans for recapitalization, purchases of problem assets, and some nationalization of banks were part of a systemwide rescue plan. Amid a weak world economy, European economic activity contracted by about 4 percent—evidence of a steep recession.

By 2010, modest improvement began to evidence itself over much of Europe, but there were significant differences among the European Union countries. A debt crisis erupted first in Greece, with threats of similar crises emerging later in Ireland and Portugal, followed by fears in Italy and Spain. With every new wave of panic, many doubted the future of both the Eurozone and the euro. Those fears, as discussed later in this chapter, have proved largely unfounded.

Amid the economic wreckage, however, opportunities began to surface. As the European Investment Fund noted in its annual report for 2011, "a crisis is also a source of opportunities since, as valuations decrease, acquisitions can be completed at more favourable prices."[2] Although the report did not mention real estate specifically, clearly the sector reflects the opportunism that often emerges after a crisis and in the early phases of recovery.

Global investors have come to Europe looking for deals on distressed property. Ireland's National Asset Management Agency (NAMA) and Spain's Sareb—both so-called bad banks, established by the government to absorb toxic assets—have portfolios of distressed loans and properties expected to be sold to investors at discounts (although perhaps not as steep as bargain hunters, particularly those from the United States, might have hoped). Among the most active have been American investors who, having witnessed the repricing in the United States, are eager to be first movers in Europe to gain a competitive advantage over those who follow.

Activity is not confined to sales of distressed properties, which began in earnest in 2013. Development, particularly in core markets, has strengthened as well. "Optimism has returned to Europe's real estate industry," the Urban Land Institute and PwC declared in their *Emerging Trends in Real*

Estate® Europe 2013 report. "Sentiment among industry leaders about the prospects for their businesses is more positive than at any time since 2008, despite the uncertain macroeconomic outlook. Equity for investment in prime commercial real estate is expected to increase, but bank debt is predicted to contract further." Although confidence is running higher within the European real estate industry, there is still caution; a full recovery, ULI and PwC noted, "is still some way off."[3]

The Good News

Although economic growth across the Eurozone has been feeble, there is good news. For one thing, the worst appears to be over. Real estate leaders interviewed for this book rated the survival of the euro and the Eurozone at about a 90 to 95 percent certainty. Looking across Europe today, it is clearly a more stable and predictable place than it was in the midst of the financial crisis. After five long, hard years with much bad news—austerity plans, rising unemployment, and doubts regarding survival of the euro—a corner has been turned. Still, real concerns remain, and the European economy will need more time to fully recover.

"Europe will be an unequal place," one senior real estate leader commented. "It's probably a reasonable bet that the currently prosperous areas will increase at a faster rate than the disadvantaged areas."

Yet even amid disappointment over what appears to be stagnating growth in Europe—which will affect real estate, particularly in secondary and tertiary markets—fears over the fate of the Eurozone have been quelled. In the West in particular, speculation about the fate of the euro and the future stability of the Eurozone had made for regular fodder in the news and on opinion pages, leading some to opine that such a political patchwork of constitutions, cultures, economies, and fiscal policies could not stand the pressure of the crisis. In the critics' view, having one currency among 18 countries with separate fiscal policies is a recipe for instability—

especially as the Eurozone struggles with high levels of debt and unemployment and weak banks.

The Eurozone got a shot in the arm, however, in July 2012 when European Central Bank (ECB) president Mario Draghi famously pledged that the ECB would do "whatever it takes" to save the euro. Another vote of confidence for the Eurozone was the September 2013 reelection of German Chancellor Angela Merkel, who became the only major European leader to be reelected twice following the financial crisis. Merkel has said Germany will continue its Eurozone policies, adding that the political victory for her party was "a very strong vote for a unified Europe."[4]

In a speech at Harvard University in October 2013, Draghi took on the critics again, specifically those based in the United States. "In the dark days of the crisis, many commentators on this side of the Atlantic looked at the euro area and were convinced it would fail," he said. "They were wrong. . . . [T]hey had underestimated the depth of European's commitment to the euro."[5]

Given the deep roots of the European Union and the widespread desire in Europe to use economic cooperation to promote stability, prosperity, and peace, one can see that too much is at stake to allow the bloc to come apart.

A Unified Europe

A comprehensive history of the European Union is beyond the scope and intention of this book. However, a brief overview provides perspective on the scope of the region, which has a population of 500 million and combined economic power of €12.5 trillion. The history of the European Union stretches back to shortly after World War II, with the creation of the Council of Europe among western European nations in 1949. By 1951, six countries—Germany, France, Italy, the Netherlands, Belgium, and Luxembourg—took the next step, with a treaty to formalize cooperation in the running of their heavy industries, such as coal and steel, which would prevent any of them from making weapons of war to be used against the other.

By the 1960s, change was afoot in Europe. The European economy had grown, helped by the lifting of custom duties among the six founding countries on goods imported from each other. For the first time, free cross-border trade was allowed. In addition, the six countries imposed the same duties on imports from outside countries, thus forming the world's biggest trading group. The 1970s saw expansion of what was then the European Community, with three new members—Denmark, Ireland, and the United Kingdom—bringing the total to nine. The community grew again in 1981, when Greece was admitted.

The 1990s saw the beginning of structural changes, with initial steps taken for the establishment of a single currency. During the decade, a single market was established—with the free movement of goods, services, people, and money—and a name change was enacted, from European Community to European Union. By the mid-1990s, the bloc was 15 members strong, covering almost all of western Europe. By the end of the decade, monetary union was adopted by 11 countries—Austria, Belgium, Finland, France, Germany, Ireland, Italy, Luxembourg, the Netherlands, Portugal, and Spain—with Greece joining in 2001.

The divisions between western and eastern Europe were later negated with the admission of eight former Eastern Bloc countries—the Czech Republic, Estonia, Hungary, Latvia, Lithuania, Poland, Slovakia, and Slovenia. Cyprus and Malta also became members. In 2007, Bulgaria and Romania joined, and in 2013 Croatia became the 28th E.U. member state.

In the five years since the onset of the financial crisis, the European Union has undertaken a significant overhaul of its financial system, including stricter regulatory standards to promote transparency and accountability. As José Manuel Durão Barroso, president of the European Commission, stated in his prepared remarks for the September 2013 State of the Union address, "If we look back and think about what we have done together to unite Europe throughout the crisis, I think it is fair to say that we would never have thought all of this possible five years ago. We are fundamentally reforming the financial sector so that people's savings are safe. We have improved the way governments work together, how they return to sound public finances and modernise their economies. We have mobilized over €700 billion to pull crisis-struck countries back from the brink, the biggest effort ever in stabilization between countries."[6]

Barroso's bold and upbeat remarks contrast with the atmosphere a year earlier when, as he recalled, there was widespread speculation, even among chief economists of many leading European banks, that Greece would leave the euro, which could have led to the unraveling of the Eurozone. "What matters now is what we make of this progress," Barroso said. "Do we talk it up, or talk it down? Do we draw confidence from it to pursue what we have started, or do we belittle the results of our efforts?"[7]

His rhetorical questions have a direct impact on the subject matter of this book—leadership in the European real estate market. Stability and improved sentiment across Europe will bolster the outlook for real estate beyond the core markets, encouraging both development and investment. As stated in Emerging Trends Europe 2013, "The past five years were about survival. But 2013 marks the beginning of the rehabilitation. For those who've made it through, it will be a year of refocusing, repositioning, and renovating. And it will be a year when survivors benefit from the release of assets to market."[8]

Leading through Uncertainty and into Recovery

Clearly, the 2008–2009 financial crisis was far steeper and more traumatic than a typical cyclical downturn. Yet, despite its extremes, the crisis had the same attributes as previous cycles and highlighted the same lessons learned, particularly regarding leverage and being too short-sighted. "As you move through a cycle, reduce exposure to leverage," advises Francis Salway, former group CEO of Land Securities Group and a longtime European real estate executive (see profile, chapter 5). "As you develop [properties], make sure you create highly desirable buildings that can attract tenants in a downturn, even if at reduced rents. Beware of obsolescence; be realistic about the reletting prospects of older properties when they get to the end of their leases."

Discernment is a vital leadership skill in real estate, and especially in Europe, given the differences among local markets. "Fragmented" is the word executives often use when describing European real estate. The most successful leaders understand the distinctions—for example, between continental Europe, with its array of cultures and economic scenarios, and the United Kingdom, which can be further divided between the strength of London and weakness in contiguous areas. There is a natural divide economically between stronger northern Europe and weaker southern Europe. Although some players do follow a pan-European strategy, it is not a one-size-fits-all approach. Real estate developers and investors need to understand the risks, potential rewards, and attributes of each locale, especially given the variability in economic growth and political stability from region to region—and even city to city.

Focus on the Cities

A strategy common among many firms, and one that will be addressed throughout this book, is the focus on major cities. This is noted by Jeremy Newsum, executive trustee of the Grosvenor Estate and nonexecutive director of Grosvenor Group Ltd. (GGL), who previously was GGL chief executive (see profile, chapter 2). He comments, "Sensible people will not think so much of a country or a region, but a city. The city markets are very different, one from another—the financially oriented Frankfurt versus the global-economy city of London, or more industrial cities in other cases."

Similarly, when Anne Kavanagh, global head of asset management and transactions for AXA Real Estate (see profile, chapter 4), looks across the map of European real estate, she sees demographic patterns and population shifts that favor the larger cities. "That's a feature across the world:

investment becomes more about cities than countries, and the dynamics of those cities," she says.

Salway concurs: "International investment is about cities, not countries, and that will become an even stronger force." Post-crisis, many investors retreated to the relative safety of the core markets—the United Kingdom, France, and Germany—and their largest cities, especially London and Paris.

A Tribute to Leadership

Whenever opportunities arise, those who have survived and succeeded over the long term will employ the same fundamentals and leadership principles that have served them well through every cycle. These are the basic lessons—avoid overheated sectors, do not take on too much risk, never use excessive leverage—that emerged previously, such as during the steep downturns of the 1970s and 1990s, and yet again in amplified form during the 2008–2009 crisis. In real estate, history has an ingrained habit of repeating itself.

Unfortunately, those who come to this sector as short-term players looking for a quick return have no historical context of previous booms and busts. They pile into real estate at the wrong time and for all the wrong reasons, paying up for overpriced assets with too much risk and leverage, hoping to get in and out before the market turns. But such an ill-conceived approach is nearly impossible to execute, leaving the landscape littered with those who tried and failed in real estate. For them, there is no cautionary tale. At the top of the next cycle it will undoubtedly happen again, with a fresh crop of short-term players. "This is an industry without many barriers to entry. Anyone with some money can buy land, build, and sell," observes Luis José Pereda, president of Grupo Lar of Spain (see profile, chapter 6).

Those who have managed to thrive and grow through the cycles are the long-term leaders who know when *not* to do something, as well as when to take action. When assets are fully priced and the risks outweigh the rewards, they have the courage of their convictions to take their chips off the table and not make deals just because they have capital available. With prudence and patience they wait for the inevitable correction to come and go, and then get back in at a much better valuation. This book is a tribute to their leadership and a showcase for their wisdom.

Real estate is a tough business that favors those with a long memory, ample patience, and the battle scars that come with experience. When the playing field is as diverse and dynamic as that in Europe, it makes the leadership principles and practices all the more important.

Notes

1. European Investment Fund, *Annual Report 2009* (Luxembourg: European Investment Fund, 2010), 12.

2. European Investment Fund, *Annual Report 2011* (Luxembourg: European Investment Fund, 2012), 13.

3. PwC and Urban Land Institute, *Emerging Trends in Real Estate® Europe 2013* (London: PwC and Urban Land Institute, 2013), 9.

4. Alison Smale and Jack Ewing, "Re-election in Hand, Merkel Moves to Form New German Government," *New York Times*, September 24, 2013, www.nytimes.com/2013/09/24/world/europe/merkel-re-elected-in-show-of-strong-support-for-party.html?_r=0.

5. Brian Blackstone, "Draghi Says U.S. Euro Critics Underestimated Europe's Political Will," *Wall Street Journal*, October 9, 2013, http://online.wsj.com/news/articles/SB10001424052702304520704579125992179402398.

6. Europa.eu, "State of the Union Address 2013," José Manuel Durão Barroso, September 11, 2013, http://europa.eu/rapid/press-release_SPEECH-13-684_en.htm.

7. Ibid.

8. PwC and ULI, *Emerging Trends Europe*, 7.

CHAPTER TWO

Adopt the Long-Term View

THE IMPORTANCE OF THINKING, ACTING, AND EXECUTING for the long term is a business cliché, but it is an essential discipline that mitigates risk, promotes stability and sustainability, and fosters an attitude of being a steward of assets in the present and for the future. No matter how obvious the virtue of focusing on the long-term view may seem, it is actually difficult to carry out because of the constant demand among some investors for higher rates of return.

Real estate development by its very nature demands a long-term view simply because the return on invested capital normally takes considerable time and patience to realize. And yet as the numerous casualties of the financial crisis of 2008–2009 have demonstrated, even some experienced real estate players can fall victim to dangerous short-term thinking. Overleverage by developers, overlending by banks to those with poor credit, and overinvestment in such high-risk instruments as collateralized debt obligations wreaked havoc on the real estate industry and the financial system. Given total, global losses from the financial crisis that are estimated in the trillions of dollars, maintaining a long-term view is not an overused phrase; it is enduring wisdom.

A Long History: Jeremy H.M. Newsum

Jeremy Newsum has been executive trustee of the Grosvenor Estate since 1993. From 1989 to June 2008, he was also chief executive of Grosvenor Group.

He is a member of the Council of Imperial College London, of Cambridge University's Syndicate for the West and North West Cambridge Estates, and a director of Grupo Lar. He is an adviser to the Al Futtaim Group. Past appointments include chairman of the Urban Land Institute (2009–2011), president of the British Property Federation (2001–2002), and director of TR Investment Property Trust (2000–2007). He was also a Church of England commissioner (1993–2000), a director of the French property company Société Foncière Lyonnaise (1997–2002), and a director of European shopping center specialist Sonae Sierra.

The European real estate sector spans centuries, as do a few of the organizations featured in this book. Thus, having a long-term perspective takes on truly historical significance. Perhaps no better example exists of the long-term view as a strategic and cultural value than that at Grosvenor Estate, with its more than 300 years of history, and its longtime leader Jeremy H.M. Newsum, executive trustee since 1993. He also was chief executive of the estate's real estate business, Grosvenor Group, from 1989 to June 2008.

Although no one in the global real estate industry has gone unscathed, and even the most successful firms have suffered their share of battle scars inflicted by a capricious market, this is a business in which longevity and a sterling reputation command respect, almost to the point of reverence. Newsum is among the leaders who have weathered the cycles over the years by never losing the long-term view. He has demonstrated the importance of remaining nimble and decisive, acting when opportunities arise but never at the expense of one's values, either personal or strategic.

"Keep an eye on those who really know what they are doing, and ignore the short-term 'glamour players' who are trying to make money very fast. There is no need to make money so quickly," advises Newsum.

Three Centuries of Grosvenor Estate

Grosvenor Estate, a privately held institution, states as its mission to "draw on our history as well as our creativity to find better ways of fostering vitality—and enduring real estate value—in the cities of today and of the future." Its vision for development encompasses "architecture, streetscapes and public spaces that future generations will value."[1]

This is not the language of the short-term speculator. Rather, this terminology conveys a sense of respect and accountability, whether to shareholders, beneficiaries, or the community at large. Leaders at Grosvenor espouse the same views, never emphasizing the quick returns of today at the expense of building a healthy and sustainable portfolio over time.

Although he distinguished himself as Grosvenor's chief executive for two decades, Newsum's early ambitions were not to plan cities or build skyscrapers. "My earliest memory is of wanting to be a farmer, and then realizing that my family didn't own a farm," he says. "So the next best thing was to be what we in Britain call a land agent, which is someone running an estate or farm on behalf of the owner."

At university, Newsum began a course of study for estate management. After the first year, he had to choose between rural and commercial; examining his prospects, he decided commercial property would be better for his future. Upon graduation in 1976, he looked for a job in London and through a friend of his grandfather was introduced to Grosvenor Estate, which provided what he called "formidable experience" in real estate. "The Grosvenor Estate has been around for [more than] 300 years in London. You can see that a decision . . . needs to be in the context of what happens long term," he says.

Grosvenor Estate is a unique British institution, encompassing the assets, business interests, rural estates, and other holdings owned by trusts on behalf of the Grosvenor family, which today is headed by Gerald Cavendish Grosvenor, sixth duke of Westminster. The Grosvenor Estate is composed of the Grosvenor Group, an international property group operating in 17 countries; Wheatsheaf Group, which has investments in sustainable food and energy initiatives; and the Family Investment Office, which includes five rural estates in the United Kingdom and Spain, an equities investment portfolio, a charitable foundation, a fine-art collection, and a historic archive. Total property assets under management in 2012 totaled £12.2 billion.[2]

Grosvenor's history is a venerable one, dating back to the marriage in 1677 of Mary Davies and Sir Thomas Grosvenor, whose family traced its roots to William the Conqueror, the first Norman king of England, whose reign began with the Norman conquest of 1066. Mary brought to the marriage an inheritance of 500 acres (200 hectares) of land north of the Thames and west of the City of London. The landholding was largely untouched until the 1720s, when development began in the northern portion—an area now known as Mayfair—around Grosvenor Square. In the 1820s, the focus shifted south to what is now Belgravia, including Eaton Square, Chester Square, and other notable locales.

Today, the London estate is managed by Grosvenor Britain & Ireland, which for the past 40 years also has managed assets elsewhere in the United Kingdom. (Grosvenor also has an office in Edinburgh.) Grosvenor has been diversified internationally for 60 years, and has a presence in the United States (San Francisco and Washington, D.C.) and Canada (Vancouver and Calgary). About two decades ago, it established offices in the Asia Pacific market, including Beijing, Hong Kong, Shanghai, and Tokyo. Regardless of locale, the common strategy across all markets is having a long-term time horizon.

For Newsum, values learned early on at Grosvenor had a significant impact on and colored his leadership over the years. "There were watchwords like 'you need to be firm but fair with the tenants' . . . and 'always leave something on the table for the other guy,'" he recalls. He also learned that a good deal is one that is not one-sided.

In 1978, after two years with Grosvenor, Newsum left to pursue his career elsewhere, working in the Savills investment team before setting

up a London office for Bidwells. Out of the blue, he was asked to return
to Grosvenor, and rejoined the organization in 1987. In 1989, at age 33,
Newsum became chief executive of Grosvenor Estate Holdings, just before
a major economic and property recession.

In the mid-1990s, Grosvenor was expanding and diversifying overseas
while other U.K. property development companies were retreating from
their overseas holdings largely because of the difficulty of running an international firm from one central headquarters. Grosvenor's modus operandi,
however, was different: it set up a structure with local boards, which allowed local decision making on investment and development. The arrange-
ment worked well for Grosvenor as a private firm, providing cohesiveness
that stemmed from it being run like a family company while decentralizing
decision making. A publicly held company, Newsum reasons, could rarely
operate in the same manner.

Although Newsum's two-decade tenure of leadership was far longer
than average for a CEO in real estate (or any industry, for that matter), he
keeps it in perspective in comparison to the very long timeline of Grosvenor Estate. On that scale, Newsum's 20-year term is only slightly visible on
the timeline—"insignificant" is the word he uses. "That is deep in the phi-
losophy of Grosvenor—that success is part of a chain, if you like, and the
critical thing is not to break the chain," he says. The objective is to make a
contribution during one's time, then pass along a company and a portfolio
of holdings that are measurably better than what was received. That is a tall
order, given the storied past and vast holdings of a company as august as
Grosvenor.

Reflecting on what makes for success in real estate, Newsum sug-
gests that it comes down to having the right mix of the basic ingredients of
ambition, the willingness to take appropriate risk, and hard work. A fourth
element is pure luck—the chance and timing of being in the right place at
the right time. In real estate, as in any endeavor, exogenous factors—from
the global economy to geopolitical risk—play a part. When the wind is at

one's back, the tasks are immeasurably easier and less risky than when there are macroeconomic or sector headwinds.

The downside, however, is that favorable conditions and timing in real estate will often drive the use of excessive leverage. This dynamic also attracts certain players to real estate who are looking to profit very quickly. Because Grosvenor Estate is owned by trusts on behalf of beneficiaries, it has responsibility for what must be preserved for posterity. That does not mean Grosvenor cannot take risks, such as speculating on a particular project or venturing into a new market, but that those risks are never on a scale that exposes the organization to too much risk. As Newsum puts it, the company accept "risks, but not a giant gamble."

Over the years, Newsum observes, those in the industry who have run into trouble often did so because they shouldered oversized risks as a direct result of thinking and acting in a manner focused too much on the short term. Pursuit of a short-term return can cause people to depart from their values. One could suppose that, in most cases, this departure is not intentional, but rather a temptation succumbed to because of the perception that there is quick money to be made.

In a 2010 editorial he penned for *Property Week*, Newsum warned against the dangers of short-term thinking and, more to the point, short-term optimism. He gave the example of the rise in U.K. property markets, stating they had returned "to one of those phases in which it is impossible to justify prices for houses and commercial investments other than on the most optimistic and short-term view of the future."[3]

The rose-colored glasses of the short-term optimist should be swapped for the clear-eyed view of the longtime realist who has seen cycles come and go and knows that values can only be justified by the economics of the transaction over the long term, he wrote. "Post-rationalisation of the prices paid by reference to investor demand, land shortage or currency translation is a fool's logic. The price of any investment property needs to be derived from its prospective rental income, and the UK's economic circumstances do not suggest that rents will be rising in any sector."[4]

In developing his views, Newsum considers himself fortunate to have worked with the beneficiary group of the Grosvenor family, defining and abiding by corporate values that are aligned with the personal and family values of the owner group. This translates into a corporate culture that emphasizes collaboration and cooperation, ensuring that those who are hired into leadership positions are aligned with and uphold those guiding principles.

Another aspect of having a long-term view is learning from mistakes. What distinguishes those who are ultimately successful is the ability to humbly admit mistakes, extract the lessons, and move on without a loss of confidence. Newsum recalls an incident from early in his career when he missed a rent review in a lease (an annual review of the agreement), which effectively closed the window for increasing rents that year. For Newsum the major takeaway was not merely learning the importance of avoiding that error again, but also noting how his boss handled it. His supervisor chalked it up to a lesson learned and was very supportive of Newsum—an experience that proved to be a very powerful example of leadership.

Over the years, not every project or deal structure has been perfect, some turning out better or worse than others. Rather than point fingers at one specific cause—or person at fault—a good leader recognizes that the responsibility ultimately rests with him or her, Newsum adds, exhibiting a level of self-reflection and accountability that comes from a long career and a balanced perspective. Such thinking is hardly confined to Grosvenor. Examples can be found across the European landscape among organizations and their leaders that place high value on the long term, adding stability to what can be a highly cyclical industry.

Long-Term Strategy as a Corporate Value

Another seasoned organization with an extensive history is the British Land Company, which was founded in 1856. Like Newsum, Sir John Ritblat, honorary president and former chairman and CEO of British Land (see profile, chapter 9), embodies the long-term view that comes from seeing cycles come and go, and riding out the worst of them.

"Most of my financial success, both corporately and personally, has been from taking the long-term view and being able to sit out the less [favorable] periods without being forced into an uncomfortable position. I think that is the most important message that I have to offer," Ritblat says. "Far too much is done on a short-term basis, and this is a huge mistake."

Establishing a long-term strategic goal also promotes creation of value as measured in total returns, which also drives the financial health of the portfolio. Development entails risks, of course, and it may take a longer period to recoup rewards. The risk/reward differential, however, tends to favor the long term.

To act for the long term, however, companies need a depth of resources that allows them to choose among opportunities and to focus on what suits them best at a given time.

That does not mean every project will be a stellar performer, and thinking long term is sometimes criticized as being stodgy or reticent to act. In fact, some firms have come under attack by investors for not being proactive enough despite having delivered solid returns over the long term. Which is more important, Newsum asks rhetorically, "is it success over the long term, or to be exposed to every last short-term opportunity which could lead to trouble?"

Having a long-term time horizon, however, does not preclude a short-term opportunistic move. As a hypothetical example, consider a parcel of land purchased with the intention of developing it. A year later, another party with a more critical need for that land offers the owner three to five times the amount originally paid. Nine times out of ten, the owner would harvest the immediate profit and move on. Making a short-term profit, however, was not the original intent; rather, it materialized in the midst of a long-term horizon.

During boom times, however, real estate has attracted players who are in it for a quick return and who seemingly forget that this is a sector that goes through pronounced cycles. Their time horizons are usually very short term and their strategies predicated on trying to make a quick profit through overleveraged risk.

Making things worse, these types of individuals typically buy a property or project with a high degree of leverage and all too often at the peak of the market, when it is overpriced. When the inevitable downturn comes, the underperformance of these projects can have devastating consequences for the developer—including loss of the project through bank foreclosure.

Long-term thinking is courageous in the midst of a boom that will inevitably be short lived. Ultimately, it is what distinguishes true leaders from the pack of followers. As Newsum wrote in *Property Week*, "Genuine pioneers in real estate are few, and it can easily be argued that throughout the last decade most decision-making among investors was about following not leading."[5]

Newsum traces the problem to the property markets themselves, which tend to be one-sided—all buyers or all sellers. "This leads to unstable markets where prices move too consistently for long periods and the lack of liquidity is easily ignored," he says.

This is all the more reason to value the long-term view, which acknowledges the cycles of the industry—both good times and bad. The good times call for a cool head and prudent thinking to keep a company from taking on too much risk or acting too aggressively in a market in which prices have been bid up to unsustainable levels. Otherwise, when the good times come to an end, so will profitability.

The Talent Equation

Long-term planning involves more than an organization thinking about its investments. It also involves talent development. Globally and across the real estate industry, one of the most pressing issues at the board level is succession planning, not only for the CEO, but also for key people at the executive level. The issue becomes more acute when looked at across an organization's leaders—executives in charge of property management, acquisitions, and/or development, as well as corporate leaders such as the chief financial officer—who in many companies may be about the same age and likely to retire within a few years of each other. (In North America, for example, leaders of real estate investment trusts, or REITs, are concerned about generational change on management teams and having a bench of talent to be developed and promoted over time into positions of responsibility.) To allay worries about talent development, companies should make succession a bigger priority, conducting comprehensive assessments of employee strengths and weaknesses.

Anne Kavanagh reflects on the generation of talent coming into the industry and whether it will be drawn more to the financial side or the real estate side, or to a combination of the two. "If I look at graduates within our business, it varies across Europe. In the States, they are all out of the business schools. In France and Germany, or the U.K., it is a mixture from the business schools or straight out of university," she says. "It is a broad mix depending on the traditions in the country and the environment."

Skill development for new talent and up-and-coming leaders means broad, cross-functional training and experience such as exposure to investment (development and acquisitions), finance, property management, and leasing. Then, as these individuals rise through the ranks of the organization and take on new responsibilities, they must acquire management and leadership skills. These skills include the ability to manage cross-culturally—a major consideration in Europe. Finally, they must develop strategic thinking. For those who will one day become a senior leader or even CEO, the twin abilities to think strategically and interface effectively with key investor stakeholders are extremely valuable.

To that end, one of Grosvenor's top priorities is investing in people, which means recruiting talent, developing skills and experience, and ensuring alignment of these people with the organization's values. Grosvenor invests in skills training for managers and young business leaders.

Reflecting on his own career at Grosvenor, Newsum speaks very positively about the contribution that can be made by an enthusiastic and innovative younger generation. To make an impact on their organizations, these young professionals need to be forthcoming about their ideas and not hold back. "If you have an idea, make sure that it is understood. Find a way to ask a question or put forth an idea. You might have to be a little clever about it because a lot of ideas get squashed," he explains.

For talent at every level, values are incredibly important—both in terms of one's owns principles and their alignment with those of the organization. "Values are important, but only if you stick to them," Newsum says. At Grosvenor, Newsum demonstrated through his long career as chief executive his alignment with the company's long-term view.

The Stewardship of the Long Term

Over the course of its long history, as Grosvenor noted in its 2012 annual report, it has been involved in the evolution of one particular city—London, its flagship city. Although the broader U.K. economy remained weak in 2012, a vibrant central London real estate market propelled the company's return from the downturn that began in 2008.

Much of Grosvenor's activity in London—about 90 percent of the portfolio value—centers on 300 acres (121 hectares) in Mayfair and Belgravia in London's West End. Neighborhoods feature a mix of owner-occupied homes, rental properties, and social housing, as well as office, retail, and amenities buildings. The occupancy rate remains high in West End at 97.8 percent, making London a safe haven for capital investment in real estate.[6]

Given its three centuries of history in London, Grosvenor Estate's property development takes on an air of stewardship to ensure viability and sustainability for generations to come. (Indeed, stewardship is a cultural value among many older, well-established firms in Europe.) Rather than engaging solely in the management of discrete property assets, Grosvenor concentrates on place making—that is, it views its London estate, in particular, as "an interlocking web of places that we seek to improve for the benefit of commercial and residential communities,"[7] it noted in the report. The approach, it added, is holistic and long term.

When undertaking development in a neighborhood where revitalization is just beginning, developers like Grosvenor project a sense of stewardship and the hope that they are making a contribution to the community. At the same time, they face significant risks; for example, a building might never reach its projected income or value. There are also tenant risks associated with development: if a large tenant leases half a building and then goes bankrupt, even though there are certain protections for the owner, a half-empty building is worth far less than a fully leased one.

Given the risks involved, the real estate business is best approached with long-term goals in mind. In the wake of the crisis of 2008–2009, the wisdom of this strategy has been proven. This approach recognizes the excessive risks involved in the pursuit of short-term goals and calls for courage of conviction in avoiding unnecessary risks such as paying excessive prices. Moreover, for organizations such as Grosvenor Estate, the long-term view is not only a way of doing business. It also preserves a legacy of leadership.

Building Blocks of Leadership

➢ Thinking long term, though it may seem like an obvious strategy, is actually difficult because of the demand for return (and increased rates of return) on a constant, quarterly basis. Yet real estate, by its very nature, is a long-term proposition. Although good leaders always have their eyes open for opportunities that emerge in the short term, they focus on long-term value generation. Leaders must remain nimble, maintaining a view to capitalize on opportunities as they arise while never overemphasizing short-term gains.

➢ It is important to know your values—personal and organizational—and their roots. A legacy does not reside in an archive; it is cultural, involving a sense of responsibility and accountability that is renewed with each negotiation, deal, and contract. The leader's values must match those of the organization, which are the fabric of its culture. This will put different demands on the leader: for example, a company with a history measured in centuries likely will have a different approach than one that was founded two years ago or one with a ten-year time horizon.

Notes

1. Grosvenor Group, *Annual Report and Accounts 2012: Living Cities*, 1.

2. Ibid.

3. Jeremy Newsum, "Property's sheep got us into this mess. A good shepherd might get us out," *Property Week*, March 2010.

4. Ibid.

5. Ibid.

6. Grosvenor, *Annual Report*, 26

7. Ibid.

CHAPTER THREE

Think Like an Entrepreneur

STRATEGIC THINKING IS A PREREQUISITE FOR LEADERSHIP, a skill without which a person's career will not advance in any industry or field. There is, however, a specialized kind of strategic thinking that enables a leader to identify opportunities before the competition can, to weigh the risks and rewards against current and projected scenarios, and to act decisively to execute a plan. That type of thinking is entrepreneurial thinking.

Entrepreneurial thinking is a leadership skill that applies globally—as applicable in the United States as it is in Europe, or anywhere else in the world, for that matter. In Europe, this thinking is applied across a patchwork of markets and opportunities—country by country, city by city, and sector by sector. In the real estate field, beyond the goal of finding opportunities is the more important objective of discerning investments providing the right fit within a portfolio and the balance between risk and reward over the long term. These tasks are accomplished largely through entrepreneurial thinking.

Within European real estate, some individuals stand out for their entrepreneurial thinking, which goes a long way to explaining their apparent knack for being in the right places at the right time. Far more than luck, they rely on proven abilities to study and analyze a host of micro- and macroeconomic factors before moving into or out of a market. Pierre Vaquier, chief executive officer of Paris-based AXA Real Estate Investment Managers, and Alexander Otto, chief executive officer of ECE Projektmanagement of Hamburg, are among the leading entrepreneurial thinkers in the industry.

The Entrepreneurial Spirit: Pierre Vaquier

With more than 30 years of industry experience, Pierre Vaquier is chief executive officer of AXA Real Estate Investment Managers Ltd., the property arm of the second-largest insurer in Europe with a portfolio worth an estimated €42 billion. Vaquier, who joined Paris-based AXA in 1993, is also a member of the AXA Investment Managers executive committee and management board. He is vice chairman of Logement Français and has been a director of Fonciére des Régions since 2001.

A 1980 graduate of HEC School of Management in Paris, he was previously director of Paribas Asset Management and CEO of Paribas Properties Inc.

A native of the French provinces, Vaquier grew up in a family that owned and managed small businesses; his father, a doctor, managed a private clinic. Although not large, these businesses exemplified how entrepreneurs discern opportunities and then nimbly respond to the local market.

After graduating from HEC School of Management, Vaquier intended to become an entrepreneur until a family friend suggested he spend one year learning about what was then called merchant banking. He joined BNP Paribas, a leading French banking and financial services company, which he describes as an organization of "people who were very innovative, risk takers, with very strong character." His one-year plan turned into 13 years with Paribas, including ten spent in the United States. In 1993, he joined AXA and became deputy CEO of AXA Real Estate Investment Managers in 1999.

Practical Yet Entrepreneurial

Real estate appealed to Vaquier because of the "concreteness" of it — "looking at very practical issues, such as location, environment, understanding how you are going to develop the surroundings." Yet even within that practical focus, there is a definite entrepreneurial flavor, of identifying opportunities and taking appropriate risks. "I like to take opportunity risk," Vaquier says. "I like the idea of . . . creating the new."

Entrepreneurial skills encompass vision, strategy, and the ability to turn a concept into reality. Entrepreneurs are idea people, seeing opportunities where others do not—or have not yet. The ability to take opportunity risk can only come from in-depth analysis that looks beneath the surface of what is visible to everyone else and beyond the headlines that form conventional wisdom. One must be willing to make decisions with incomplete information—and usually without the comfort of the crowd. That does not mean taking on a huge amount of risk. Rather, entrepreneurial thinkers gather the facts and make their own conclusions, which may make them contrarian at times. Entrepreneurial thinkers have vision and the ability to devise and execute a strategy to bring that vision to reality.

Entrepreneurial thinking improves discernment, particularly in finding opportunities that are a strategic fit for a company—and for the long term. "In the development business, there are so many different opportunities at any one time, so you really need to concentrate and focus on the right ones," says Otto (see profile later in this chapter).

Ideal timing is predicated on making a move early enough, but also on having the confidence that the fundamentals are favorable. Vaquier gives the example of investing after a downturn, such as was experienced in Europe in the 1990s. "When there is a major adjustment, you need to have strong support for the turnaround. There is no need to act in advance. When the market is turning around, you will have time to seize the opportunities," he says.

Discernment applies not only to entering a market, but also in determining when to pull back. For example, in March 2013, AXA Real Estate announced it was reducing its exposure in France because of concerns over the economy caused by the tax policies enacted by French President François Hollande, including €20 billion in tax increases to counter a budget deficit. An article in the *Financial Times* quoted Vaquier as saying France was suffering from "a conjunction of issues" that made it less attractive for real estate investment. "The fundamentals of the economy are poor," he added, noting that a "lack of comprehensive reform" compared with other European countries had led him to conclude that France "is becoming a middle-of-the-pack economy." Among his arguments, he cited increases in the country's capital gains tax, which, he said, could hamper efforts to attract investors for the medium and long term. "That is bad for the fundamentals of real estate; we see challenges in terms of higher vacancies and a lack of rental growth," Vaquier said.[1]

Although France will remain a core market, AXA Real Estate began to shift its focus to opportunities in Germany, the United Kingdom, and Scandinavia.

Finding Opportunities

Looking across Europe, Vaquier provides an assessment of opportunities, both in markets that have been strong, such as London and Paris, and in those that appear to be turning around, such as Spain. The first factor to take into consideration, he says, is the improvement in the stability of the euro and declining currency risk. In mid-2012, currency risk in the euro was pegged at 20 to 25 percent; a year later, it was 5 percent, he says. (Other European real estate leaders concur, saying Germany's continued support of the euro demonstrates the likelihood that the monetary union will remain intact.) As currency risk has been reduced, some opportunities have opened to re-explore markets such as Spain. "A year ago [2012], Spain was no good, regardless of the price of the assets there, because of the currency risk. Today, there has been a big evolution," Vaquier says.

When it comes to overall economic factors, though, Europe remains clearly delineated between north and south, with northern Europe continuing to show stronger economic growth than southern Europe. In general, the north is regarded as safer and the south as riskier. Because of its economic risks, Vaquier puts France today "in the camp of southern

Europe," whereas he previously considered it part of the stronger northern European region.

Risks in the southern European market do not preclude making investments there; rather, opportunities must be evaluated accordingly. "If you look at southern Europe, you will look at it opportunistically, but you will also be demanding good pricing—and you will try to acquire proper-ties where there is not as much risk in the short term," Vaquier explains. "In the northern part of Europe, we have a preference for a more value-added strategy because we see the economy as having more visibility and higher growth rates, which enable us to take a bit more risk." Add in the fact that prime areas in Germany and the United Kingdom for real estate remain rather expensive (in part because of increased interest from Asian investors), there may be more of an impetus to take on additional risk in northern Europe by investing in secondary markets in order to gain return.

Geography is not the only thing Vaquier and other entrepreneurial thinkers see when they look at Europe. Industry sectors, too, vary within and across borders. "You look at the business models of your tenants—storage, logistics, this sort of thing," he says. "A lot of sectors are evolving." One example is the rising demand for space to house sophisticated data centers. Within the retail sector, Paris remains a hub, bolstered by its strong tourism draw, while that sector is softer across the rest of France.

No matter where or when an investment is to be made, Vaquier returns to the basic criteria that are the benchmark for any transaction—price and the expected return. In high-risk and low-risk environments alike, entrepreneurial thinking comes down to judgment calls based on the way one assesses the business environment, economic climate, job growth, sector strength, political regimes, demographics, and more. Not every investor will see things the same way; varied opinions and perspectives are what make a marketplace. "It creates opportunity, because some parts of the market are mispriced," he says. For the entrepreneurial-minded, the key is to always have one's eyes open and ears to the ground to identify the opportunities as they arise.

Going Deep into the Fundamentals: Alexander Otto

Alexander Otto is chief executive officer of ECE Projektmanagement GmbH & Co. KG of Hamburg, an investment and development firm that specializes in developing, building, managing, and leasing retail real estate. It also develops and builds transport and logistics centers, corporate headquarters, and other office and industrial buildings, railway stations, and other special-purpose properties. Founded in 1965 by his father, Werner Otto, ECE is the European market leader in urban shopping centers.

Alexander Otto obtained his international baccalaureate at Oxford University and continued his studies at Harvard University and Harvard Business School. He joined ECE in 1994, and in 2000 was appointed CEO. Under his leadership, ECE expanded from its dominance in Germany to being the European market leader in the shopping center sector. The company has developed projects in 16 countries, operating a €26 billion portfolio of assets under management. ECE has become a leading developer and service provider in the field of office and special-purpose properties.

Otto holds a seat on the supervisory boards of the Otto Group and DES Deutsche EuroShop AG, and is a member of the advisory board of Peek & Cloppenburg KG in Düsseldorf. He is chair of the International Council of Shopping Centres (ICSC) Europe and the advisory board of ULI Europe, and is a board member of the Harvard Business School Foundation of Germany.

He is the major shareholder in Developers Diversified Realty (DDR), a leading U.S. shopping center company that develops and manages properties across the United States and in Puerto Rico, Brazil, and Canada.

He is the founder and chairman of the board of trustees of the Lebendige Stadt (Vibrant City) Foundation, which has as its mission revitalization of Europe's city centers, and of the Alexander Otto Sportstiftung Foundation, which funds youth sports and facilities.

From the time Otto took over as CEO of ECE Projektmanagement in 2000, he has continued the company's legacy of strong growth that began under his predecessors. Retail real estate has been a significant part of that growth, as evidenced by the 200 shopping centers in the ECE portfolio today, up from 60 when Otto took the reins of the company. Like others profiled in this book, he attributes growth and success to finding "good projects" and looking beyond short-term development opportunities. "Only develop projects that are really viable for the long term," he advises.

Developing retail real estate has diversified ECE's portfolio geographically, allowing the company to pursue its goal of market dominance. Rather than focus only on large cities, ECE has been willing to go into secondary markets where it sees opportunities to develop retail space without the level of competition that would be present in a prime market. "We have a lot of good assets in secondary cities," Otto notes. "Often, it's better to have the dominant asset in a secondary city than a number-five asset in a strong city."

With such a significant retail presence, ECE has closely watched the shifts in that sector and its impact on the real estate portfolio. Following a growth phase in retail development over the past decade, including a development boom in eastern Europe, the tone in the sector today is more cautious. Now, the focus is on consolidation as retailers "right-size" their operations in order to make them more efficient and well-suited as concepts for the future.

A trend that ECE watches closely is the growth of e-commerce. As industry figures show, e-commerce has been gaining ground globally, increasing the competitive threat to bricks-and-mortar locations. According to an A.T. Kearney study, global e-commerce grew by 13 percent annually from 2006 to 2011, from $214 billion (€161 billion) to $399 billion (€300 billion). "Retail expansion is increasingly occurring through online channels as a way to tap into growth markets, build brands, and learn about consumers while investing less capital than traditional formats,"[2] A.T. Kearney reported.

"There is a lot of concern and caution in the retail businesses, with a lot of changes occurring," Otto says. "The growth of the internet is one of the biggest challenges that retailers are focusing on, particularly in electronics and book retailing."

Understanding Consumers

In order to understand the current and projected impact of e-commerce on the retail market, ECE joined with Roland Berger Strategy Consultants, in collaboration with the Otto Group and Union Investment, to delve more deeply into trends in consumer behavior. Beyond its insightful conclusions, the resulting study itself is significant as an example of how an entrepreneurial thinker seeks to understand an issue firsthand in order to inform strategic decisions rather than rely on the opinions and conclusions of others. In any field, organizations cannot rely on the conventional wisdom to govern their decision making. Having a finger on the pulse of the most important markets allows nimble, entrepreneurial firms to act with market intelligence. In ECE's case, rather than sift through the endless debate and media headlines, it made a significant commitment of time and resources to engage in original research and analysis of the European retail sector.

The retail study painted a multifaceted picture that challenged several assumptions, especially that traditional off-line retailing has become a dinosaur and that e-commerce will dominate in the future. "The debate about competition between online and traditional offline retail has been dragging on for a long time now. The same arguments are traded back and forth again and again. . . . But for all the tiresome discussions, few tenable conclusions have been reached [with regards to] the future," the study stated. "It is therefore high time to throw a few fresh insights into the mix: First and foremost, competition within and between sales channels ought to result in better offerings for the consumer. It also opens up a whole host of opportunities for retailers and manufacturers, both online and offline."[3]

One conclusion to be drawn from the study is in the frequently evoked buzzword *multichannel*. There is no single way to reach all consumers all the time for all their purchases. "If it turns out that the customers do indeed shop in multiple channels, the next question is: Why do they buy certain products in one channel rather than the other?" the study asked. "Where customers mainly want to save time, online and offline channels should be integrated in a 'click-and-mortar' constellation that benefits customer convenience."[4]

With its tremendous retail assets, ECE undoubtedly takes some comfort in the study's compelling arguments suggesting that offline retail remains firmly anchored in the consumer world. Traditional retailing enjoys several edges over online retailing, including significantly higher sales volumes, higher purchase frequencies, a broader mix of products in the shopping cart, and higher levels of spontaneous buying. At the same time, however, online retail continues to grow—and faster than many observers had expected. "The online retail world can be likened to a hydra: it has many heads, but each is of a different size and poses a different level of risk to offline retail."[5]

Whether a business is a retail outlet or a real estate developer building shopping malls, understanding customer behavior is critical to assessing whether one's current strategy remains relevant to business conditions or whether adjustments have to be made. Indeed, relevance occupies the minds of most entrepreneurial thinkers. "We saw that quite a bit of euros are being spent already over the internet—that there is a certain substitution" of e-commerce for a visit to a retail location, Otto says of the study's findings. "However, there has been no sales erosion in our centers as yet." As time goes on, though, the mix of retailers may shift in response to evolving consumer tastes and shopping practices.

"The challenge for each of the big players in the shopping center business is to manage the business efficiently and in every market," Otto says. For that kind of responsiveness, the business strategy must be flexible and adaptable to accommodate the changing tastes and evolving consumer habits in the local market.

Acting Locally

For any entrepreneurial operation, a close connection with the local market is imperative. In real estate development, that means having the right local teams that are able to gather market intelligence and undertake fact-finding, and which may also be empowered to do at least some degree of decision making. "We are in 16 countries. The way we manage our business is to find good, motivated local teams who have contact with international retailers and also national ones," Otto says.

Managing an international organization that acts globally as well as locally is essentially a "people issue." The key to success is building an effective team. Even the most gifted idea generator will not succeed as an entrepreneur unless he or she can scale the business through other people. A perfect example is the European real estate company that works in various countries—across multiple languages, cultures, and social norms. This diversity is a distinguishing factor of the European real estate market, and far different from developing and investing in properties across the 50 U.S. states or Canada's ten provinces and three territories. To manage within such a diverse cultural fabric, successful European real estate companies rely on local teams (further addressed in chapter 4) that provide companies with "boots on the ground," as well as greater cultural sensitivity.

"You need to have some clear guidelines that must be followed companywide. But there are some things that need to be done individually in certain countries," Otto says, such as assessing opportunities and getting aligned with the local business climate.

Relying on a local presence also places high importance on the ideas and input of others, whether they are members of the senior leadership team or associates in the field. "What distinguishes good leaders is they are truly good listeners. They *really* listen. They might not always agree with you, but you can see them filtering what you say into their thought processes and how they look at the world and how they should act," observes Jon Zehner, global head of Client Capital Group at LaSalle Investment Management, based in London, and a member of LaSalle's global management committee (see profile, chapter 4).

The cyclical nature of the real estate market elevates the importance of gathering a variety of informed viewpoints. Without them, it is difficult

to detect early signals indicating a shift, whether a turnaround or deteriora-
tion in market conditions. "When you stop listening to others and to the
marketplace, you convince yourself that you have some kind of formula
that works forever," Vaquier says.

From a management perspective, strategies and priorities must be
continuously refined and communicated to the team. This fosters cohesion
among team members and creates alignment behind the strategy.

How a company organizes itself will vary from one organization to
another. An important commonality, though, is entrepreneurial thinking.
This means paying close attention to the signs and signals that confirm a
trend or indicate a shift. Although no one, entrepreneurial-minded or not,
has a foolproof crystal ball, those who do well in business—and in real
estate, in particular—are those who pay the closest attention. They listen
intently, study the marketplace, do in-depth analysis, and keep an open
mind.

Great leaders rely on strategic instincts to uncover factors that affect
their business—both what is visible on the radar screen today and the
trends just beginning to emerge. They look beyond the immediate and
ask themselves where the opportunities are likely to be tomorrow. In short,
they think and act like entrepreneurs with a vision rather than dealmakers
whose focus is limited to one deal at a time.

Building Blocks of Leadership

➤ Entrepreneurial thinking means focusing on the new and different but
never losing sight of the risks, whether across a region or country or within
a specific sector. As Vaquier observes, "The risks impact the way you want
to deploy your capital." Risks and rewards are weighed on a case-by-case basis, taking macro- and micro-economic factors into account. The entrepreneurial thinker gathers facts broadly, especially by listening to others—and
in particular to those closest to the marketplace.

➢   The entrepreneurial thinker recognizes that opportunities come from market knowledge at the consumer level. To discern the trends, it is not enough to listen to the pundits or read the news. For example, in the case of ECE, the leading developer of shopping centers in Europe, it makes sense that its market-intelligence focus must be on the retail consumers who frequent bricks-and-mortar stores, as well as those who shop online. Primary research will yield insights that may run counter to conventional wisdom, or add depth and nuance to it.

Notes

1. Ed Hammond and Scheherazade Daneshkhu, "AXA to Reduce its Exposure to France," *Financial Times*, March 24, 2013, www.ft.com/intl/cms/s/0/b1f606c0-9486-11e2-9487-00144feabdc0.html.

2. A.T. Kearney, "E-Commerce Is the Next Frontier in Global Expansion: The 2012 Global Retail E-Commerce Index," https://www.atkearney.com/paper/-/asset_publisher/dVxv4Hz2h8bS/content/e-commerce-is-the-next-frontier-in-global-expansion/10192.

3. Roland Berger Strategy Consultants and ECE Projektmanagement, *What the Customer Really Wants: The Truth about Shopping in a Multichannel World—Opportunities for Retailers and Manufacturers*, 2013, 5.

4. Ibid., 37.

5. Ibid., 19.

CHAPTER FOUR

Be a Mapmaker, Not a Map Reader

IN THE AGE OF EXPLORATION, European explorers and cartographers put brush to parchment to redefine the known world. They did not simply retrace the lines made by others; rather, they pushed the boundaries of human exploration and knowledge.

In many ways, today's real estate leaders are like those explorers and cartographers of old. On a literal level, their plans and projects put new lines on maps—from the streets of subdivisions to redeveloped urban spaces and altered skylines. On a figurative level, visionary real estate executives change the map of urban areas and reinvent how things are done. They find ways to collaborate across cultures, balance technological connection with old-fashioned face-to-face communication, and push beyond old boundaries to embrace the new reality of what it means to be pan-European.

Two leaders who have become skilled explorers and mapmakers, comfortable with a clean canvas and setting their own courses, are Anne Kavanagh, global head of asset management and transactions for AXA Real Estate, and Jon Zehner, global head of the Client Capital Group for LaSalle Investment Management. They are among the real estate leaders who navigate an industry that continues to evolve. In their successes, they model the adaptability needed to be comfortable with the dynamic of continuous change.

Leaders in real estate today must have the confidence to trust their instincts while knowing that at times they will make mistakes. Even if they have to (figuratively) erase and redraw part of their maps, they are undeterred in their quest for opportunity and, ultimately, success.

The Pan-European Leader: Anne Kavanagh

Anne Kavanagh is the global head of asset management and transactions for AXA Real Estate, based in London. With 27 years of industry experience, Kavanagh joined AXA in 2010.

Previously, she was managing director, real estate, for Lazard in London, and was head of real estate, Europe, for Cambridge Place Investment Management. Before that, she was an international director in the European capital markets business at Jones Lang LaSalle.

Kavanagh studied urban estate management at Nottingham Trent University. She is a chartered surveyor and a trustee of the Urban Land Institute.

It takes a particular set of navigation skills to maintain an intense focus on the local market while also pursuing a broader business strategy that looks for opportunities across Europe—and perhaps even around the globe. These are the complexities and nuances of running a pan-European real estate operation. How, then, do leaders gain such expertise?

For Kavanagh, mastering the pan-European market—and the global market as well, given her responsibilities as head of global asset management and transactions—has been achieved through her more than 25 years in European real estate.

Kavanagh came from a family of academics and wanted to pursue a degree in geography (which seems entirely fitting for a "mapmaker") until her family asked where these studies would lead. Unsure of how to respond, she switched to pursuing a degree in real estate. After completing her degree, Kavanagh spent a year working in the industry, and discovered it was a great fit. As she told *Urban Land* magazine, "When I first started working in the early '80s, you were never in the office. I was out of the office a lot in my first job, inspecting properties and visiting towns and factories. It was an interesting way to connect with the world."[1]

To add to her skill set, she followed what was then the standard route for professionals in the British real estate industry, pursuing accreditation by the Royal Institute of Chartered Surveyors. (Kavanagh compared the accreditation method to that for chartered accountants.) She became a chartered surveyor as a result of joining the graduate program at Jones Lang Wootton (predecessor to Jones Lang LaSalle) in 1983. "You had to cover areas such as valuations, construction, and investment. It was a broad-discipline approach, and you were not just put into one department that offered a narrow experience,"[2] she said.

Over the course of her career, Kavanagh has worked in an advisory role, for a hedge fund, at an investment bank, and then in her current position with AXA, through which she returned to the investment management side of the business. "Each role has brought a different dimension, and without each previous role, I wouldn't have been able to do the job I was doing," she says.

Early in her career, Kavanagh specialized in London real estate, which she calls "a fabulous market in which to have your first experiences." Over time, she moved into broader roles, which allows her to see a landscape that is rife with enormous challenges yet brimming with significant opportunities. Indeed, the ability to home in on both aspects of the terrain—the inherent risk and the promise of reward—is crucial to success within or across markets.

The Banking Sector Challenge

Biggest among the current challenges is the European banking sector, in which new capital and liquidity rules for banks could result in a multi-trillion-euro funding gap over the next several years. In *Emerging Trends in Real Estate® 2013 Europe*, the Urban Land Institute and PwC noted, "The economic outlook remains unsettled. Europe still faces about €400 billion of deleveraging risk. And banks . . . are undertaking a structural reduction of their commercial real estate lending."[3] The need for banks to reduce their exposure to real estate is structural rather than cyclical, and the impact could be felt for the next ten years, she says.

In the interim, there is likely to be an "unprecedented sale of assets," Kavanagh says. As banks sell holdings to raise capital—most likely at deeply discounted prices—investors who have access to capital will be poised to scoop up bargains. Thus, dealing with what is highly problematic on one level will yield opportunities in the real estate sector on another. As *Emerging Trends* stated, "Wherever one sits in the market, there is an expectation of greater asset sales by lenders this year." Among the respondents to the 2013 survey for *Emerging Trends*, 66 percent identified the pending asset sales as the "biggest business issue," which "foreshadows an increased deal flow for those able to act." As one respondent to the survey noted, "Over recent months, we have seen banks writing down assets at prices closer to buyers' expectations. For those assets that are outside of the core space, they are getting valued lower by the day; it's in this market that the bargains will be found."[4]

As the leaders interviewed for this book note, sales in Ireland held by the National Asset Management Agency, in particular, will attract bargain hunters. Ireland set up NAMA as what has been dubbed a "bad bank" to manage distressed real estate assets with a face value of €74 billion; it plans to liquidate the assets over ten years.

Seeking the Extra Return

Another aspect of the European map of opportunity is an increased appetite for higher returns, albeit with extra risk. Although activity in the more predictable core markets remains solid, Kavanagh says there has been increased interest of late in markets outside the core to generate extra return. "So, for example, will Moscow become more important in the next ten years? Yes," she says, but cautions, "it's not a focus for investors today."

Returning to the mapmaker metaphor, while the cartographers of old populated the fringes of their charts with fearsome monsters, intrepid real estate executives are willing to explore the possibilities outside the core areas, but with a careful eye on the risks. Regardless of where opportunities are sought, a variety of macroeconomic factors must be taken into account, including demographics, which, in general, continue to favor the larger cities; immigration policies; and e-commerce and its impact on retailing and store locations (see chapter 3).

"All of these things are playing out in real estate at the same time as the dislocation of the markets," Kavanagh says. "Activity is speeding up. The trends that in the past took five to ten years to play out are now playing out in 12 to 18 months."

The Local Team

When opportunities surface, it takes a team to realize them. "We have teams on the ground in ten countries in Europe. Being close to the market and having relationships that are deep in those markets are important components to doing business," Kavanagh says. "You have the overlay of different countries—language, culture, legal system, governmental dynamics. How do you factor all that in?"

The answer is the local team, which does not necessarily mean those who were born in a particular country, but definitely those most fluent in both language and familiar with the culture. "In our Paris office, for example, we have people who grew up in Paris, [though they] weren't born there. The same in Germany. You really want people who are embedded in the local community and who have the language skills and the cultural understanding to function well in that marketplace," she adds. "You can fly some people in and out, and you can have a group of people who are moving around the organization and doing pan-European roles. But fundamentally, you have to work with local teams."

Whenever a company has a network of global offices, including in Europe, one cannot discount the fact that bonds and affinities tend to develop among people of the same backgrounds and cultures. People who have these commonalities typically like to work together. Therefore, companies that have, for example, French speakers and people who are French by background have an easier time doing business in France. The same holds true for Germany and other countries.

At the same time, fluency with language and culture creates a pan-European environment with which members of the younger generation of talent, in particular, seem particularly at ease. They can move cross-culturally, provided they possess the right language and cultural skills. As an example, Kavanagh cites AXA's analyst pool of French, Italian, Swedish, and German professionals who work across the business. "That's what this younger generation is all about," she says. "It's like my children: they think of themselves as pan-European."

To run a truly pan-European business, people at the top need to be sensitive to the variety of cultures and backgrounds spread across the map of where they do business. These differences include such things as legal and tax structures, bank regulations, the way people buy consumer goods, how industrial goods are shipped, and the formalities of how offices and apartments are leased. There is no all-purpose way to get things done, and anyone who tries to impose his or her own way of doing things on other countries and cultures will fail.

Possessing or developing a depth of cultural sensitivity takes a particular mentality or aptitude—cultural DNA. Significant challenges can exist within an organizational structure between senior executives who are running markets such as France or Germany, or even regionally between those running northern Europe and southern Europe. Irrespective of location, they must relate to each other, forging bonds across cultures—a dynamic that requires a distinctive skill set and strong leadership. "The difficulty that you often find in real estate is that the leaders who are . . . good dealmakers are not always the best managers. It's the same in other businesses such as investment banking," Kavanagh notes.

Despite these cultural challenges and the nuances of doing business in several countries, the pan-European terrain does make doing business today relatively easy, thanks largely to a common currency across most countries in the European Union. But there are other changes as well that make connections easier to forge, Kavanagh observes. "It's probably easier to do business today, in relative terms, than at any time in the last ten years. It's easier to move around the markets, thanks to the transportation connection." Years ago when Kavanagh started traveling to Sweden on business, there were only two flights a week from London. Now there are multiple flights every day. "Now you can move seamlessly from one country to another or around the globe," she says. "I was in three cities in Canada last week."

The Values Compass

While a company may have a mosaic of cultures and backgrounds among its people, there is a need for strong, personal alignment with the cultural values of the organization, which is true not only in real estate, but also in any industry. "That means personal leadership that is aligned with organizational values," Kavanagh says. "This is important because the scope for misunderstandings across cultures is huge."

An example of where such miscommunications can occur is in e-mail, which tends to be made up of truncated messages in which tone and intent can be misconstrued, particularly across cultures. "We are communicating more, but we may not be understanding or listening the way you think," she says. Thus, while e-mail is a time-saver, it may not be as productive in the long run if it leads to misunderstandings or disagreements that need to be ironed out later. "In a pan-European business, we are doing a lot of face-to-face. But you need to get the right balance of that to be efficient. I don't know any successful pan-European business that isn't looking at putting its people together on a regular basis."

Whether traversing north to south or across the decades, there are certain constants for the explorer/mapmaker. In real estate leadership, these fixed points are the core values of trust, integrity, and putting the needs of clients first. Unfortunately, when a business sector heats up and new entrants are attracted to the profits to be made, values can sometimes be compromised. "At the peak of the cycle, there were groups that weren't focused on relationships and trust and integrity—what you could call the 'historical values,'" Kavanagh notes.

Blinded by the promise of big returns in a short period of time, some people pursued opportunities aggressively, which resulted in over-development, overleverage, overexposure—over-*everything*. The lesson to be learned in the aftermath of the financial crisis of 2008–2009 is never lose your moral compass. Traditional, longstanding values are crucial to weathering the storms and keeping an even keel through the cycles. "If you look after your clients and do the right thing by them, you should always be okay," Kavanagh says.

A Global Executive Surveys the Horizon: Jon Zehner

Jon Zehner is global head of Client Capital Group for LaSalle Investment Management, based in London. He is responsible for leading LaSalle's global activities relating to capital raising, new product development, merchant banking, and large-scale, cross-border strategic investments with partners. Zehner is also a member of LaSalle's global management committee.

Zehner joined LaSalle from AREA Property Partners, where he was a senior director. Before joining AREA in 2009, he spent 28 years with JP Morgan Chase & Co., where he held a number of senior positions, including global head of real estate investment banking and head of sub-Saharan Africa.

He is an active leader in a number of industry organizations, including serving as chair of the Real Estate Advisory Board of the University of Cambridge and as a trustee and member of the board of directors of the Urban Land Institute. Previously, he cofounded and served on the executive board of the European Public Real Estate Association (EPRA).

Zehner is an American. If there were ever any doubt of that, his accent would give him away, he quips. And yet this London-based real estate executive deserves a place among leaders in the European real estate industry because of his experience and perspective working in the United Kingdom and on the continent, and in many other corners of the globe as well. In fact, although he does not fully embrace the label, he is probably best described as a global executive—as his title, global head of the Client Capital Group at LaSalle Investment Management, attests. "I'm often told that I'm an unusual American," Zehner says. "I am just as comfortable in Japan as the U.K. I don't think of myself as global, but the truth is I'm not so far from it."

Thinking Globally

His global perspective makes him representative of the kinds of people who are successful. Regardless of where they grew up, they have purposefully experienced different parts of the world. When it comes to being pan-European or global, they walk the talk of cultural appreciation and understanding.

Zehner is also among the explorer/mapmakers in the industry, literally exploring new territories and emerging markets. A prime example is when, after spending several years in both London and New York City for JPMorgan, he moved to South Africa in 2005 to run the company's sub-Saharan Africa business. "The chance to be in an emerging market and to manage 600 people was compelling," he said.

It also proved to be a strategic move, coming as it did at a time when the real estate market was getting overheated. Today, having worked in real estate on three continents—North America, Europe, and Africa—Zehner has developed an almost scholarly discipline as he studies not only the current dynamics of the market, but the history behind it.

For example, he explains how, in the 1990s, South Africa experienced a banking crisis, after which it adopted policies that translated into a very tight grip on lending in the country. As a result, while the United States and many European countries saw too much lending by banks in the mid-2000s and mounting leverage in the system, South Africa neither got overextended during the boom nor was hit with the full impact of the crisis. Applying lessons learned elsewhere to real estate markets such as in Europe is a mark of a true explorer/mapmaker.

Over the years, Zehner has been very involved in the European real estate industry as a founder of the European Public Real Estate Association (EPRA), a member of the Real Estate Advisory Board of the University of Cambridge, and a board member of the Urban Land Institute. Such activities enhance Zehner's global perspective. Like Kavanagh, he is able to take a step back and survey the landscape for both opportunities and challenges while operating both globally and within local markets.

Broader Economic and Political Issues

Looking at Europe today, Zehner says the issues are not merely "real estate questions," but rather broader economic and political questions. At the top of the list of concerns are economic growth and job creation, which are fundamental underpinnings of real estate activity. Next on his list are the debt markets, which, as noted, have not stabilized. "Banks still have significant problems, there is no public [debt] market to speak of, and in mezzanine debt, although there are more new entrants, there is a shortage of that debt," he says.

Kavanagh, meanwhile, foresees a change in the European debt markets, which historically have been dominated by banks. Going forward, she predicts, European debt markets will become more like those in the United States, with institutional players accounting for 20 percent or more of the market.

Furthermore, even when the Eurozone crisis is out of the headlines (or, more realistically, is replaced by a host of geopolitical concerns of the day), it is never far from globally minded leaders in real estate. For instance, Greece, which has been a hotbed of dissent and public protests over the European Union's austerity plan, has debt that is reported to be about 170 percent of its gross domestic product. Spain, Portugal, and Ireland also have been on the Eurozone radar as problem areas and have come under pressure to narrow their budget deficits. However, in late 2013, an expected change in European Union budget rules was expected to ease the austerity requirements for some countries, particularly Spain.[5] The reelection of German Chancellor Angela Merkel was seen as an endorsement of her strategies for managing the Eurozone and left little doubt that the euro, itself, would survive. In France, meanwhile, the government has been criticized for not dealing head-on with its fiscal problems because of concern over social issues. And on it goes . . .

These brief summaries are but a small and cursory sample of the concerns real estate leaders must be well-versed in as they set their priorities globally and regionally, and execute them locally. "The world is getting to be so complex and intertwined," Zehner says. "Real estate leaders, going forward, will have to figure out what's happening to the euro, what's happening to weaker countries in the Eurozone, what's the level of economic growth, what's happening to the banks . . ."

And yet, risks and challenges notwithstanding, Zehner considers himself an optimist. "If you look at the investor flows in real estate — and I believe this is true more broadly, as well — Europe has become the flavor of the year. The U.S. is regarded as good, but fully valued. Asia is okay, and investors are refocusing their attention there. But the amount of capital coming into Europe is amazing to me. . . . The prospects for the region are not as dire as people had thought. Clearly, there are still significant issues, but it feels very much like Europe has turned the corner."

As the competitive landscape of European real estate shifts and morphs, leaders in the industry must become intrepid explorers/mapmakers, rather than map readers relying on past knowledge. With vision and confidence, they gauge the terrain and take appropriate calculable risks in pursuit of a reward that, they hope, will make the voyage worthwhile.

Building Blocks of Leadership

➤ Being an explorer/mapmaker means having the self-confidence and conviction to go your own way, believing that you will end up at the right place. This is not about bravado, but rather instinct and experience. The explorer/mapmaker/entrepreneur will face the unknown and expects uncertainty, but is not daunted by it. This is the challenge that provides motivation to find opportunity. As the saying goes, if you're not the lead dog, the view never changes. Only from the front, as the leader and not a follower, can you set your own course, on your own terms.

➤ Explorers/mapmakers cross boundaries and span cultures, but they never stop respecting them, as well. They understand and appreciate the differences from country to country and culture to culture, and remain sensitive to them. Their teams include people who speak the languages and observe the cultures of the places in which they do business. Having a global mind-set is no excuse for not appreciating diversity and uniqueness.

Notes

1. Stephen R. Blank, "Evolution of a Global Leader," *Urban Land*, July/August 2013, 93.

2. Ibid.

3. PwC and ULI, *Emerging Trends Europe 2013*, 7.

4. Ibid., 12.

5. Matthew Dalton, "Austerity Seen Easing with Change to EU Budget Policy," *Wall Street Journal*, September 19, 2013.

CHAPTER FIVE

Go Your Own Way

AMONG LEADERS IN ANY INDUSTRY, there are innovators and risk-takers who are willing to "go their own way" in pursuit of opportunity—particularly an opportunity that is ahead of the curve. Akin to the entrepreneurial thinker described in chapter 3, these independent-minded people take a slightly different tack: they seek to be the early movers after a downturn or to make a calculated bet in a new or recovering location after thoroughly analyzing the risks. Believing that most, if not all, of the downside is behind them, they anticipate the probability of at least a slight improvement that will yield a modest return—and the potential for healthier gains and a much larger return.

Many of the real estate leaders profiled in this book exhibit such traits. Two, in particular, are Francis Salway, who recently stepped down as group chief executive officer of Land Securities Group, and Roger Orf, who has a long history as an investor in European real estate and is currently partner and head of European real estate for Apollo Global Management. Both are based in London. As these two real estate leaders exemplify, the willingness to go your own way takes both vision and courage.

Independent Minded: Francis W. Salway

Francis W. Salway was group chief executive officer of Land Securities Group plc from July 2004 to March 2012.

He joined Land Securities, the largest publicly traded property company in the United Kingdom in terms of market capitalization, in October 2000 as head of the portfolio management team, with responsibility for its investment portfolio. He led the Land Securities development team in May 2002, with responsibility for its program throughout the United Kingdom, and in January 2003 became chief operating officer of Land Securities Group. Previously, he served as an investment director at Standard Life Investments.

He has been an independent, nonexecutive director of British retail chain Next Plc since June 1, 2010, and in the mid-2000s was a director of London First, a nonprofit organization dedicated to making London the best city for business. He also was a nonexecutive director of Investment Property Databank Ltd. before its sale to MSCI.

In 1986, Salway undertook a year of research at the College of Estate Management, culminating in publication of the book *Depreciation of Commercial Property.*

Independent minded and a seeker of opportunities, Salway considers himself a contrarian who is willing to take risks because he believes "you can do something that makes a difference—and has an impact."

Going his own way is a theme that has run through Salway's life and career. From the beginning he has seized opportunities and shouldered responsibilities, but never with a shoot-from-the-hip mentality. His modus operandi has been to study all the variables and model the outcomes, both positive and negative. He does not mind setting off on a solitary path (fitting for someone whose pastimes are hiking and mountain climbing) but is never unprepared.

Looking back on early influences, Salway discusses his father, who ran a small professional firm and managed farmland and forestry for clients. Salway, however, never aimed to join his father's business, even though that is what his father might have preferred. "I wanted to be my own man," he says. "I never wanted to be seen as having inherited something. I wanted to do it for myself."

Early Years

Salway's first job was as a surveyor trainee at CB Richard Ellis. Later, he joined Standard Life in Edinburgh, where he was a fund manager for eight years. During his time there he was given full responsibility for the performance of two property funds, an experience he found highly motivating. "I realized then that nobody was holding me back," Salway says. "I realized that if I was successful, I would be able to take credit." (One of the funds he managed was a number-one performer over a five-year period.) "That, for me, was a seminal moment because property, to a degree, is an investment business. Yes, there are operational sides to the business, and, generally, listed property companies get more involved in the operational side than the more passive investors. . . . But whether it's individual leasing transactions, acquisitions and sales, or corporate activity, these are investment decisions."

The Standard Life funds he managed at the time held direct property assets; they held no securities. Other activities included a small amount of development work, as well as funding of development projects. By funding others' projects, Salway learned, it was possible to finesse the timing after others have endured the early, more uncertain stages of a development when "you can never quite be sure when it will all come together." He adds, "A lot of development is about timing."

Through the experience of running the two funds, Salway gained a lasting appreciation for effective leadership that empowers others by giving them "deep responsibility and opportunities to make things happen." This became a tenet of his own leadership, particularly during his years at Land Securities. "I constantly questioned whether we were giving young people at Land Securities enough responsibility early on. I would sometimes say to my colleagues on the executive board, 'Are we now giving people as much responsibility as we might have had when we were in our early 30s, when we got a break?'"

Orf agrees. A key part of real estate leadership is imparting knowledge to the team. "I never would have been as successful as I've been if I hadn't taught people who were half my age how to do business," he says.

For both men, leadership and developing others stem directly from remembering the opportunities they pursued in the early stages of their careers. For Salway, one promising endeavor emerged unexpectedly during his days working in development and seeing buildings demolished after only two or three decades. "I thought, if the guy who developed that building had known it was going to be knocked down in 25 years' time, how would that have impacted the numbers in his appraisal at the beginning? I had been spending ages just playing around with numbers and then, suddenly, I read a small article that a university was looking for somebody to do a year's research project on this precise subject. And I went for it!"

The result was a project undertaken at the College of Estate Management in 1986, which culminated in the publication of *Depreciation of Commercial Property*. Nearly 30 years (and many distinguished accomplishments later), Salway spoke with pride about that research project and the risk he took in undertaking it. "My expertise was around the drivers of property returns, but I had to write about accounting treatment depreciation, which was then highly controversial because it [discussed] a new accounting standard that had been implemented after years of debate. . . . And then, a year later, out pops this young guy who is going to write a book on the subject matter, including a chapter on the accounting treatment of depreciation."

Suddenly, young Salway found himself in the spotlight. For someone so young to understand so well the complexities of accounting principles and the impact on property depreciation was extraordinary. Since then, Salway has kept a lively interest in academic pursuits—including serving as a visiting professor at the London School of Economics and chairman of its

Real Estate, Economics, and Finance Advisory Board—which allows him to meet and converse with senior academics.

Described as cerebral, Salway is clearly a deep thinker, particularly as he discerns opportunities and undertakes investments early in the cycle. For example, he followed his "research first and act accordingly" model immediately after the downturn of the early 1990s, when rental values had fallen by as much as 50 percent. Not only were rents lower, but also long-term leases (25-year leases had been the norm in the United Kingdom until that time) now had "break clauses everywhere."

Within that dynamic, Salway and his team found an opportunity by employing cash-flow modeling—essentially looking at what would happen if tenants exercised the break clauses in their lease agreements and, as a result, buildings became partly vacant. "So it was pricing shorter lease duration and the risk of vacancies," Salway sums up. Understanding those variables, he and his team bought a number of buildings "at very low rents and very high yields because nobody else would touch them because of the lease breaks." Because of their willingness to go their own way at a turning point in the market recovery, they earned an unleveraged annual return on those properties in the range of 25 to 30 percent.

Salway credits such a healthy return to a willingness to take on risk that might scare off others. This boldness allows entry into new or recovering areas, but only after all the variables and risks are uncovered, studied, and understood—a sense of discipline that must be emphasized today in the wake of the most recent global crisis. "Now that there is so much information about forecasts and rental growth in different markets around the world, it should logically be priced in," he adds. "But I do think that risk is sometimes mispriced. And, it is mispriced at the peak of the market and it is mispriced at the bottom of the market."

The ability to seize opportunities that others cannot, or will not, is not only at times contrarian, but also opportunistic. This is the courage displayed by investors and developers who are willing to go their own way without the comfort of acting with the crowd. "Be prepared to do bold things that create competitive advantage when you are clearly doing something earlier than others," Salway advises.

The independent-minded contrarian also knows when to get out of a market, no matter how good it looks to others. For example, in a previous role in the 1990s, Salway was managing properties in Ireland at a time of very low interest rates. Perceiving a bubble forming in the Irish economy, Salway decided to exit the properties in the late 1990s. That bubble continued into 2007, followed by a massive collapse in property values and a spate of nonperforming loans. "That gives you a feeling of just how extreme some of the distortions were in some of the European countries," he says. "It was the right call, but years early on the timing."

Whenever heightened risks or changes in trends necessitate a shift, the leader must set a compelling strategy and communicate it clearly to others on the team. "Setting a path and energizing people are all part of leadership," Salway says. Without such communication, a leader may choose to go his or her own way, but the team may be confused or reluctant to follow.

The Land Securities Strategic Path

Land Securities specializes in office and retail space in London and throughout the United Kingdom. "We made a decision, which we periodically reviewed, not to expand internationally," Salway says. As a specialist in its segments, Land Securities enjoys a market share of 4 to 6 percent—a percentage that would constitute a small presence in other industries, but that in real estate it is actually large and significant. Over the years, Land Securities at times has accounted for about 20 percent of development activity in the London office and shopping center markets. "When we thought the time was right, we made quite a push on development," Salway explains.

For example, in January 2010, following the global crisis, Land Securities was the first to restart a large development program in London office properties and also reentered shopping center development. This is a prime example of a contrarian move, which also earned praise. An article in the *Telegraph* on Salway's legacy after eight years as chief executive noted that "Salway's response since the chaos of 2008 and 2009 may turn out to be his greatest achievement. After restructuring the balance sheet, Salway started the biggest development programme in the U.K."[1]

Land Securities developments were the first projects of significant scale at that time, targeted to fill a gap Salway foresaw in new office and retail space caused by a lack of bank financing for developers following the crisis.

For Salway, being first or among the first to act after a downturn has been a hallmark of his leadership. As the *London Evening Standard* observed in early 2010, when Land Securities announced three projects totaling £655 million, it was "the first significant move by a blue-chip developer, the first serious sign of life returning to the property sector—a signal that the economy could be on the way back."[2] The projects were a shopping center in Leeds, an office development in London's West End, and the so-called Walkie-Talkie skyscraper in London, a 37-story building that earned its name from its shape and sloping sides. The Trinity Leeds shopping center was the biggest new mall to open in Britain after the recession and was two-thirds leased or under offer two years before it was due to open.

The move was also courageous, given the harsh impact the global crisis had on property development and investment companies in Europe and around the world. As Salway told the *Guardian* in an interview in early 2011, "Even when we were still in the low point of the downturn, our board committed to not being risk averse as we moved into the recovery phase. We made sure we had a strong balance sheet."[3]

When the time is ripe, a successful move proves to be not only advantageous, but also a bellwether of positive change. Timing requires attention to the smallest of details, indicating that a shift is at hand. "When you decide 'this is a big shift,' you go for it . . . and do as much as you can, as quickly as you can."

The Veteran Dealmaker: Roger Orf

Roger Orf is a partner and head of European real estate for Apollo Global Management, a New York City–based private equity firm. He oversees all property investments and acquisition activities on behalf of Apollo's real estate funds throughout Europe. Apollo acquired Citi Property Investors, the real estate investment group of Citigroup. Orf had been European president and CEO of Citi Property Investors.

Before joining Apollo in 2010, Orf spent the majority of his career investing in European real estate. He is also a founder of E-Shelter GmbH, a Germany-based data center business.

Orf is chairman of Urban Land Institute's ULI Europe for the 2013–2014 term. He is a member of the University of Chicago Graduate School of Business global advisory board and the visiting committee for the University of Chicago Law School. He serves on the Georgetown University board of regents. He holds JD and MBA degrees from the University of Chicago, as well as a BA in economics (magna cum laude) from Georgetown University, where he was a member of Phi Beta Kappa.

The ability to strike out on a path of one's own design and choosing is honed with time and experience, and involves weathering the storms and knowing when change is in the air. For Orf, a well-regarded veteran dealmaker, being opportunistic today is grounded in the wisdom gained during previous cycles. "This is my third cycle. I'm a veteran of this," he says. "I think this one is the best from a buying-opportunity perspective."

Orf's first downcycle was in the 1990s. At that time, Orf, who was born and raised in Missouri, moved to London from New York, where he worked for Goldman Sachs. After that first downturn, he found ample opportunities to invest in European real estate. Then came the downturn of 2000 when he was, in effect, investing for his own account as he capitalized on buying opportunities. Although he terms the crisis of 2008–2009 the "most miserable" by far, today it is yielding opportunities in the availability of very attractive deals, particularly as distressed properties are sold at bargain prices. "It's going to be great for the next five or ten years to participate in this because I think there's a lot of activity," Orf says.

As of late 2013, Orf has been focusing on secondary assets because many investors have been reluctant to commit to buying outside of prime markets in London or Paris. For those like Orf who are willing to go their own way, secondary markets offer the possibility of earning a healthy premium. "We've gone from literally doing nothing for five years by way of actual acquisitions to being extremely active," he says.

Whereas many investors focus on prime areas of London, Orf looks at the British investment landscape differently, seeing strategic opportunities in areas that are accessible to and from London and that offer a higher yield than can be found in the center of the city. He gives the example of properties in London that might produce a 4 percent yield, whereas others in Redding, Slough, or Maidenhead, which are a short distance from London by train, may yield 10 percent. "Same covenant, great buildings, great location, but there's a premium for buying office properties in the center of London," he explains.

That is not to say no risks are involved, even when assets are bargain priced. However, deep discounts compared with replacement cost make many acquisitions very attractive, even when there is little or no rental growth.

For example, Apollo Global Management recently completed a very large nonperforming loan deal in Ireland, paying €200 million for assets with a face value of about €1 billion—a drastic discount from the underlying book values of loans spread across residential, office, and retail properties. Other recent investments have been made in Zone 1 in London, such as buying apartment buildings in Kensington and South Kensington and then refurbishing them to be leased at material increases in rents. Apollo has also purchased office properties at Heathrow Airport (known as the M4 Corridor).

As a buyer, Apollo Group also has been active in France, where it purchased a large logistics portfolio, and in Germany with the purchase of office properties. In general, buying such secondary assets takes advantage of what Orf sees as mispricing and, therefore, the opportunity to earn a higher return than that available from primary assets. "So if you buy a well-located asset in a town [outside of London] or a similar type of town in France or Germany, chances are the yield will be 300 to 500 basis points higher than what it would be in the center of [a city]," he says.

Activity in the European sector has been spurred by aggressive selling by financial institutions that are throwing in the towel, capitulating to sell at lower prices. Banks and funds are prepared to clear the decks because their balance sheets have been sufficiently strengthened, allowing them to sell at a loss rather than continue carrying underperforming assets. Willing sellers, coupled with early signs of recovery and debt markets that are slowly opening up, have changed the dynamics for opportunistic buyers.

Bargain Hunting in Strategic, Secondary Assets

As noted in chapter 1, hunting for bargains, like European real estate investing in general, must be done on a case-by-case, country-by-country, and even city-by-city basis. While secondary assets in the United Kingdom appear attractive, there are secondary markets elsewhere in Europe that have been very slow to recover. Spain, for example, has seen little activity because of concerns about solvency and the impact of austerity measures. Nonetheless, Orf sees potential for Spain because of its desirable attributes—sun and a pleasant climate. Thus, Spain is an example of a secondary market suffering from illiquidity that will, at the first glimmer of improvement, appeal to buyers who are willing to provide liquidity in return for the potential for strong returns. Staying one step ahead requires foresight and nimbleness—or, as Orf describes it, "being clever enough to pull off deals that someone else may not get, or being able to see around corners and getting into potential opportunities that people aren't prepared to commit their capital to as yet."

Orf explains that his firm has been prepared to buy on an all-equity basis, based on its belief that growth in property values will resume—if not this year, then next year or the year after. "It's a question of whether the glass is half empty or the glass is half full," he says. Clearly, for those willing to go their own way, the glass is half full, with opportunity and potential. Risk remains, of course, but often accompanied by price discrepancies that bode well for favorable corrections.

Voicing an opinion echoed throughout this book, Orf sees demographic trends putting much of that opportunity in cities. London, for example, is expected to see its population grow by 14 percent by 2020, topping 9 million, thanks to immigration and rising birthrates. "Around the world, people from the countryside move to the cities. I'm a perfect example of that: I'm a small-town boy who wanted an opportunity to leave that small town," he notes.

"On an absolute level, maybe the overall population of 320 million Europeans will remain about the same. But on a relative basis, there are population shifts, either defined by household growth or by people moving. You can participate in this trend through making investments in the path of growth."

In addition to investing in residential and office properties in anticipation of population shifts and job growth in cities, Orf sees retail as "the most dynamic of the asset classes" because consumers' tastes are always changing. "I'm still getting my suits from the same place on the West End, but the way my kids shop is drastically different," he observes.

Even as the internet and e-commerce continue to affect retailing, Orf believes there will be ways to participate in this sector because, no matter how consumers make their purchases, goods still need to be transported from a manufacturer to a store or to a consumer's home. "We're quite happy to invest in logistics because we think that's an area that will continue to grow."

Long Days and Hard Work in Pursuit of a Return

For those who go their own way, leadership is a full commitment—of long days and hard work in pursuit of a return. Moreover, as noted earlier, developing talent is an essential part of leadership in order to improve the competency of the team and to ensure that a deep bench of talent exists to move into the upper ranks of management. "There are people here who have been working for me, in some instances, for more than a decade," Orf says. "Why have they done that? Partly because they learn, partly because they grow in profit terms, and partly because they respect what I've done."

As Salway and Orf demonstrate, leaders who do well do not go it alone as they make calculated bets at crucial times—such as early in the recovery phase after a downturn or when opportunities are about to emerge. These leaders rely on the strengths and talents of their teams, especially those on the ground in local markets, who become valued contributors. Hubris that causes leaders to ignore their team members, particularly those who voice concerns about escalating risks, is usually a fatal flaw.

Led by a seasoned leader who has been through downturns and upsets before, and who possesses the wisdom that comes from past victories as well as battle scars, a cohesive team can pursue opportunities for current positioning and future growth. "Part of the reason these leaders have been successful is they're able to communicate to a very loyal team," Orf says. "These leaders see opportunity where other people see danger. And sometimes danger and opportunity intersect."

At that intersection, for the experienced leader at the helm of a talented team, is an invitation to go his or her own way—at a time when and into places where others are unwilling to venture.

Building Blocks of Leadership

➤ Developing others is a key component of leadership—expanding the depth and breadth of the talent bench. Giving people opportunities to learn new skills and take on additional responsibilities is an excellent way to develop both competence and confidence. Leaders who have gone their own way in their careers typically have a personal appreciation for this developmental step, remembering the opportunities they were given earlier in their careers. As the head of their own firm now, these leaders are keen to ensure that their team members are given plenty of opportunities to stretch and prove themselves.

➤   It takes experience, vision, and strength of leadership to strike off on a path of one's own design—and to lead others along that route. In European real estate, veteran leaders have weathered previous cycles and have experience reducing risk on the downside and identifying opportunities early on as conditions improve. Those who are going their own way after the 2008–2009 crisis, for example, are drawing on previous experience to identify opportunities in areas such as distressed assets that are being sold at bargain prices.

Notes

1. Graham Ruddick, "Francis Salway Leaves a Clear Legacy at Land Securities," *Telegraph*, January 24, 2012.

2. Chris Blackhurt, "Land Securities' Francis Salway Is Laying the Foundation for Recovery," *London Evening Standard*, January 27, 2010.

3. Julia Kollewe, "Land Securities Boss Is a Safe Pair of Hands with a Skyscraper," *Guardian*, January 28, 2011.

CHAPTER SIX

Think Globally, Act Locally:
An International Perspective

FOR MANY EUROPEAN REAL ESTATE LEADERS, success is derived from core markets—those traditional strongholds of expertise and profitability. This approach was affirmed after the global financial crisis, which prompted many firms to reduce their international exposure because of the risks involved. But not all retreated. Many firms have retained a broader, truly international perspective. Among those firms are Germany-based Allianz Real Estate and Grupo Lar of Spain, which under their leaders have taken an international view that is distinctively both personal and professional.

For Olivier Piani, chief executive officer of Allianz Real Estate, and Luis José Pereda, president and chairman of Grupo Lar, an international strategy is a natural offshoot of their personal backgrounds and education. Both studied in Europe and the United States, as have other European real estate executives. In addition, both work at firms with geographically diverse portfolios—in the case of Grupo Lar, spanning the Eastern and Western hemispheres. Yet, as noted in earlier chapters, the objective is always to act locally.

Differences from market to market, as already discussed, involve not just tax codes and property laws, but also nuances that may not be so apparent or obvious to the uninitiated. Time and again, European real estate leaders voiced the need for local talent, particularly people who demonstrate an entrepreneurial mind-set as well as specific skill sets, whether in transactions or finance.

Yet the globally minded executive benefits from having broader horizons—figurative or literal—whether seeking opportunities in diversified markets or gaining from the lessons learned in other regions of the world.

Globally Minded: Olivier Piani

Olivier Piani is chief executive officer of Allianz Real Estate, one of the world's leading property investment and asset managers, with strategic management in Munich and Paris.

Previously, Piani was president of GE Real Estate Europe and general manager of GE Real Estate France. He joined GE from UIC-SOFAL in Paris. Before that, he was chief financial and administrative officer at Paribas North America, a financial services company. He also was a deputy chief financial officer at Becker Paribas, worked in the financial management division at Banque Paribas, and was a consultant at McKinsey.

Piani is a board member of UIS, the loan institution of Paris-based Altarea Cogedim. He has been a member of the supervisory board of Foncière des Murs since 2006, and is a member of the supervisory board of Cogedim S.A.S. He was also a representative director of Bail Investissement SA.

Piani received an MBA from Stanford University in 1981 and an undergraduate degree in business administration from École Supérieure de Commerce de Paris in 1977.

From the beginning, Piani has had a global perspective. His father was born in New York and his mother in Morocco; Piani, though, considers himself French, by birth and heritage. His professional life includes working in Paris, London, and New York City, with firms such as U.S.-based General Electric (GE) and now Germany-based Allianz, which has strategic management offices in Munich and Paris. "So my whole life has been, one way or the other, influenced by diverse cultures, diverse languages, and diverse entities around the world," Piani says. "That's an important trait in the sense that I'm not just a Frenchman, but a European citizen with a strong North American influence."

Adding to his international view, Piani's early mentors were global professionals, the first being his father, who was a senior executive for a large French chemical company, a position that involved much travel and dealing with constituents worldwide. Another was an American executive for a San Francisco–based paper company for whom Piani worked just before enrolling in business school at Stanford University. "So my desire to understand the world and different cultures started with my father and was also influenced by this American gentleman I had met," he adds. As one who benefited from mentoring early on and as a mentor later in his career, Piani places high value on mentorship.

With a foundation based on early international connections, Piani navigates the complexities of European markets across multiple languages and cultures. This requires flexibility and adaptability, not only on the part of the individual, but in the organizational culture as well, as Piani experienced when he joined Allianz. When he was recruited to join Allianz from GE, Piani told the company of his desire to live in Paris for the sake of his wife and three children. Although this could have proved challenging or even been a barrier to hiring him, Allianz accommodated Piani's request, which speaks volumes about the value the company saw in him.

Piani sees the company's decision as a reflection on its astuteness in understanding the nuances of running a truly pan-European operation. "They are quite smart when it comes to the way Europe works and what you need to have to make it work," Piani says. "They hired the best they could find for a given position, not the best they could find in Munich or the best German person."

Being French allows Piani to work closely with French companies on behalf of Allianz. "Because I am French and I speak French to them, doing business this way makes sense," he explains. Moreover, he brings to the job a proven understanding of what it means to do business not only in France, but also in Italy, Switzerland, Spain, and other countries. "It's much easier if you have a diverse upbringing, understanding, and feel for it," he adds.

Piani's latest career move would not have been possible, however, if Allianz had not taken a pan-European view and sought a chief executive that matched that perspective. "I'm very grateful, because I was hired by a company based in Germany to become the global leader for real estate—a job that previously had not existed, and a job that meant taking all the different real estate departments and interests in companies around the world and bringing them together in one organization," Piani says.

Allianz's objective was to build a real estate practice that is truly global in scope, capitalizing on opportunities to invest in and manage real estate assets. The firm is composed of a group of insurance companies in Germany, France, Italy, Switzerland, and other European countries. Currently, it holds about €23.5 billion of real estate assets around the world, with a loan portfolio worth about €6.6 billion, bringing its total exposure to real estate to about €30 billion. Most of the assets are in Europe, and 90 percent of its equity assets are European. On the loan side, however, five out of six of its loan activities are based in the United States.

Sixty to 65 percent of its assets are office properties, followed by residential, largely in Germany, France, and Switzerland. Overall, the residential sector accounts for more than 20 percent of the Allianz holdings; the remaining portion consists of retail, logistics, and other assets.[1]

The Pan-European Strategy

As seen across European real estate, an important leadership ability is cultivating a pan-European and even global perspective. Many of the most successful executives, regardless of personal background, have invested in their own multicultural development. Piani believes such an approach is crucial to success in European real estate which, by definition, is a collection of local markets. One cannot impose on the market of one country the business model or way of transacting business in another.

"Real estate is a local business. You have to build it respecting the local interests," Piani says. "The best people to find the right investments in Paris, for example, are not the Americans, the British, or the Germans; they're French. And so for every country, you need someone to devise a strategy, control the business, measure the people, and so forth. It must be local, or as local as possible."

While being responsible for managing the local business, key talent in specific countries or markets must also interact with the organization's leaders, who may be located elsewhere. In addition, local talent must have the ability to work across borders with other colleagues. A company may work with a retailer in a major market—for example, Germany—that is now moving to another location, such as Portugal, Brazil, or Turkey.

Looking ahead, Piani sees opportunities for Allianz to grow in three areas. The first is by increasing its presence outside Europe so that its non-Eurozone holdings increase to 20 percent of its total assets from 10 percent. "Proportionately we will grow more outside Europe than in Europe, and mainly I am referring to the U.S. and/or Asia,"[2] Piani said.

The second growth objective is to increase its retail exposure from about 10 percent to 20 percent within the next three to five years. Third, Allianz is looking to expand the way it does business, increasing its involvement with partners or funds.[3] As the company executes this growth strategy, Piani will bring to bear his uniquely global point of view.

Understanding People: The Universal Truth

Global leadership, in Piani's view, comes down to two things: understanding people and managing them—and in that order of importance. By understanding people, leaders develop the cultural finesse needed to connect and communicate with them. An understanding of what motivates people, what is meaningful to them, how they define success, and so forth, fosters more effective management. "In real estate and finance in particular, . . . it's just a question of people," Piani says. "Yes, real estate is a [physical] asset of bricks and mortar. But the success you have over time in real estate is by growing individuals to where they reach their potential."

Other leaders concur. Patrick Kanters (see profile, chapter 7), shares a global perspective, having run European and Asia Pacific real estate for APG Asset Management, where he is managing director, global real estate. "I think leadership success is very much about teamwork, and assimilating your team members and accommodating your team members so they can flourish," he observes. "Helping them perform at their best is all about setting clear goals and creating an environment that promotes a very positive mind-set, which promotes being entrepreneurial. At the same time, the leader has to make sure everybody is heading in the right direction."

In an examination of successful leaders in European real estate, and more broadly across global industries, certain universal traits stand out. These enduring characteristics produce strong leaders with longevity in their fields. Asked to reflect on these attributes, Piani names "knowing yourself" as the most important—an ability that not all leaders and managers (and those who aspire to these positions) possess. Moreover, self-knowledge is not something that is easily learned in university or business school, but it can be developed with introspection.

Hand-in-hand with self-knowledge is authenticity or, as Piani describes it, simply "being yourself"—a pursuit he often recommends to young people. "I tell them, there's no point in trying to imitate someone else, whether a stronger person you have seen or a leader. It doesn't work like that. You can learn from others, but you must be yourself. The notion of accepting, knowing, and being yourself is very important."

With self-awareness comes acknowledgment of one's weaknesses and need for development in particular areas to enhance one's leadership. Such an acknowledgment, even to oneself, requires a good dose of humility—the understanding that past successes and accomplishments offer no guarantee for the future. The willingness to learn, ultimately, separates those who reach a plateau of competence and those who continue to grow and excel.

"I think people can learn, but you have to be in the right environment," Piani says. "As we grow, we learn. If you had asked me 25 or 30
years ago whether I would be running an investment management company today with 450 people around the world and more than €25 billion
in assets, I don't know what I would have said. But I've grown into that role
in the way I've lived and in the evolution of what I've done from a professional point of view. Now, I see it as my responsibility to build and create
this environment for the next generation of leaders."

An important point is that those learning experiences have occurred
in a global context. One particular scenario into which Piani was thrust
carried responsibilities that, as he can now see clearly, were beyond his
capabilities at the time. And yet, by taking on the challenge, he expanded
his skill set and demonstrated his commitment to do whatever it took to
achieve an objective. In 1984, while Piani was working for Paribas, the
French real estate market was in poor shape, and, suddenly, U.S.-based
assets that had performed well took a downward turn. Piani was sent to the
United States to work out an agreement to sell a group of assets.

"I was 30 years old at the time, and I spent 40 days and nights negotiating," Piani recalls. "It was a job ten times bigger and more important than
anything I had ever done before or was prepared to do. But I guess I rose to
the occasion."

Beyond any particular skills Piani developed (for example, honing
his expertise in negotiating), he learned firsthand the importance of seizing
growth opportunities. The experience also influenced how he leads and
develops others. "If you're a smart and hard-working professional, there are
hardly any limits to what you can do," he says.

Furthermore, stretching oneself requires the willingness to "change
before you have to," Piani says, quoting GE's iconic former CEO Jack
Welch. "These simple words mean a lot because change is everywhere.
Refusing to see or embrace change is not a good strategy because then it's
going to get you."

Piani sees resistance to change as an attitude that is "more European than American," adding, "A lot of people complain in Europe, especially these days, about change." But as he sees it, change often brings opportunities to do something new. "Look at change as the driver of what you're going to do next."

From Europe to Latin America: Luis José Pereda

Luis José Pereda is president and chairman of the board of Grupo Lar, a Spanish multinational company that combines investment and development with property asset management. He began his career at Banque National de Paris and joined Grupo Lar in 1984.

Grupo Lar, which is privately held, was founded in the 1970s and is one of the largest real estate developers in Spain. It also has a presence in Romania, Poland, Germany, Mexico, Brazil, Peru, and Colombia. The company is 80 percent controlled by the Pereda family; another 16 percent is controlled by the Special Situations Fund.

The core of Grupo Lar's activity is the development of, investment in, and management of real estate assets, including primary and secondary residences, shopping malls, offices, and industrial parks.

Pereda is also a member of the international advisory board of Hypothekenbank Frankfurt Aktiengesellschaft, an adviser to the board of Barceló, and a member of the advisory committee of the venture capital group GED.

For Pereda, opportunity in real estate is viewed through a global lens. His company, Grupo Lar, spans eight countries in Europe and Latin America and has its sights on other markets, as well. "Currently, we have more than 2,000 apartments under construction in different markets that are growing," Pereda says.

Like Piani, Pereda developed his international perspective early. After studying economics and law in Spain, he received a master's degree from the University of Navarra and continued his postgraduate studies in finance at the Massachusetts Institute of Technology. After his studies, Pereda was

invited to join a small company owned by his father and three partners
that specialized in a niche real estate market—investing in old buildings in
Madrid whose leases were rent controlled over the long term. Moreover,
the leases were allowed to be passed from one generation to the next—as
many as three successive generations in one apartment with rent that was
basically frozen. Because the cash flow from the leases was limited, the
buildings could be purchased very cheaply. The company would then try
to sell the building to the tenants or give them an indemnity and sell the
property on the open market. "After a couple of years, I told my father that I
didn't see much future in that business," Pereda explains.

The business evolved, and by 1986 a new, small company was formed
by Pereda, his father, and a brother, which soon expanded into residential development. After their father's retirement, Pereda and his brother
expanded the company into the 1990s, which were not easy times for
residential development. Later in the 1990s, the business became involved
in commercial development, working with investment funds. For example,
early projects included shopping centers and office development in part-
nership with Goldman Sachs.

"To be honest, we were learning as we were doing," Pereda says. "But
that's how the company began to grow."

Later, the Special Situations Fund invested in Grupo Lar and now
has about a 16 percent stake. Thus capitalized, the company began an international expansion, first in Mexico, then in central and eastern Europe,
and finally in Brazil, Peru, and Colombia. "We had a pretty good eight to
nine years, from 1998 to 2006," Pereda recalls.

Then, the global crisis hit, the aftermath of which has been especially
long lasting and painful in Spain, where the economy is stymied and property values have suffered. Spain's unemployment rate, at more than 25 percent, is the highest in the industrial world. Spain suffered from 2008 all the
way through 2013 with repeated bouts of recession due to the European
debt crisis. In Spain, the crisis was triggered by defaults on loans, a crash
in its real estate market, and the bankruptcy of several major companies.

Lately, there have been signs of improvement, but the road to recovery remains long. In late September 2013, Spanish Prime Minister Mariano Rajoy told the *Wall Street Journal* that Spain had emerged late that summer from more than two years of recession but still faced a long period of more austerity. "Spain is out of recession but not out of the crisis,"[4] Rajoy said.

Another hopeful sign for the country's economy has been activity by at least one very notable investor: Bill Gates reportedly paid €108.5 million for about a 6 percent stake in Fomento de Construcciones & Contratas SA, making him the second-largest shareholder in the Spanish construction company. Spanish officials called Gates's investment in Fomento de Construcciones modest in monetary terms but symbolically important as showing foreign investors' "trust and credibility" in Spain.[5]

Survival in a Hard-Hit Market

As a Spanish company that has focused traditionally on the Spanish real estate market, Grupo Lar has demonstrated the discipline to strengthen its balance sheet and mitigate risks in one of the markets hardest hit by the global crisis. "We have a healthy cash position, and that's the best thing I can say," Pereda says.

One of Grupo Lar's most notable accomplishments is that it is among only a few Spanish real estate firms to survive. The health that Grupo Lar enjoys today resulted from its defensive posture during the crisis, shrinking its operations in Spain and selling its business in Paris. "We survived for three or four reasons," Pereda says. "One is that we never went into a big purchasing spree in Spain like others did. We didn't buy a lot in 2006." Not only did the company stop buying early on, it also stopped building. "We had no cranes in Spain after November 2006," he adds.

Second, more than one-third of its land transactions in Spain were options-based. Thus, when the crisis hit, Grupo Lar could decide not to exercise its options, losing relatively small amounts of capital rather than

suffering the massive declines in asset values it would have had it purchased land outright.

The third reason for its survival, Pereda says: "We have a strong financial discipline." The Grupo Lar holding company has no debt and provides
no guarantees to its investment vehicles. With no recourse to the holding
company, the organization was in excellent shape to weather the storm.
Now, it is poised to act opportunistically as devalued properties and assets
are sold by a government agency, Spain's Sareb.

Similar to NAMA in Ireland (see chapter 4), Sareb was established
by the government as a "bad bank" to take foreclosed property and nonperforming loans off the hands of the weakest Spanish banks. The plan,
according to reports, is for Sareb to sell real estate debt and properties over
the next 15 years; these assets were acquired from nationalized lenders at
deep discounts for €50.8 billion. A first deal from Sareb, known as Project Bull—the sale in August 2013 of a majority stake in a package of 939
homes to a Miami-based private equity firm—was closely watched.[6]

"The Sareb is selling portfolios of all kinds of assets, including real
estate and loans. Some prices, we think, are pretty attractive," Pereda says.
"Obviously, many people are also seeing that, and there is a lot of competition. Many of the international real estate funds are very focused on that."

More recently, as fears over the Spanish economy have subsided, investor interest has returned. "There is a hypothesis that Spain will recover,
which will eventually reduce unemployment, and the debt market will
normalize," Pereda says. "Then people will begin to rent or buy again. You
have to believe in that hypothesis. We also believe Spain will improve. In
fact in Europe, I would say most of our focus is in Spain."

Madrid is viewed by many as the most attractive market in Spain.
Once again, the theme is that focusing on specific cities is a key to success.
As noted in *Emerging Trends in Real Estate® Europe 2013*, some inter-
viewees were optimistic about prospects in Madrid. "As long as Spain does
not go bust, Madrid is starting to be an interesting market, with very good
absolute prices in yields and rents."[7]

The Diversified Hedge

Although Grupo Lar has been very active in Spain over the years, it has retained a global perspective, which has provided opportunities to grow, along with the safety net of diversification. For example, as the Spanish market weakened substantially, other countries in which Grupo Lar has been active have performed well. In Latin America, the Brazilian market was very strong all the way into 2009. Peru and Colombia have also done well, and Mexico, in general, has had a positive economic performance. And while some eastern and central European countries, including Germany, experienced declining markets, they were offset by good performances elsewhere, such as in Poland.

For Grupo Lar, Latin America continues to be a central focus of its activity—investing, buying land, financing, and building. "At least 75 percent or even more of our efforts financially and in terms of activity is in Latin America," Pereda says. There, too, Grupo Lar follows a "specific city strategy," targeting Bogotá, São Paulo, Mexico City, and Lima. "Most of our investment is among those four cities," Pereda says. "Each has its own dynamic."

Knowing the World Takes Research

Taking a worldwide approach requires far more than stabbing one's finger at a spinning globe. It requires in-depth research because, as both Piani and Pereda note, the attributes and nuances of each market are different, even from one country to its neighbor. "We put a lot of effort into that research," Pereda says. "I dedicate more than half of my time to trying to understand that dynamic. That is key in our business."

Every quarter, Grupo Lar reviews its markets, dedicating about a day to each city or market area. Of that time, about half is dedicated to analysis and the other half to planning—activities that must be undertaken separately, Pereda says. "We also have advisory boards that give us better insight into each of the cities. And we hire local talent. . . . We try to behave like locals as much as we can."

Echoing a comment by Piani, Pereda emphasizes that models from one country cannot be imposed on another because the risks always differ from place to place. "Absorb as much as you can from the environment, but every hypothesis that you are using has to be tested again and again," he says.

For those who take a global perspective, acting locally remains the secret to success, particularly in a business that is volatile and very risky. While ideas can be shared and the lessons learned in one place may apply elsewhere, approaches and strategies must always be tailored to the local market. In that way, a global reach can be extended to capitalize on opportunities while the risks encountered along the way are minimized.

Building Blocks of Leadership

➢　Thinking globally while acting locally is a necessary balance in real estate. An international perspective broadens one's horizons. New and diverse opportunities may emerge in one market that provide growth in the portfolio while other markets are static or even declining. At the same time, successful real estate leaders know that one cannot impose norms from one market onto another. Yet by taking a broad, international view, one develops a multicultural perspective that enhances leadership.

➢　An international perspective requires in-depth knowledge of market dynamics, culture, and ways of doing business in diverse markets. Global leaders in real estate who have been successful devote a great deal of time, energy, and resources to research in order to understand the differences in dynamics from market to market. Local teams and advisers are invaluable for gaining insight into specific markets, enabling a company to act locally no matter where its headquarters are.

Notes

1. Allianz Real Estate News, "An Interview with Olivier Piani, CEO, Allianz Real Estate," July 12, 2012, www.allianz-realestate.com/en/press/interviews/07-12-12-interview-with-olivier-piani/.

2. Ibid.

3. Ibid.

4. Richard Boudreaux and Christopher Bjork, "Spain Emerges from Recession but Sees More Austerity Ahead," *Wall Street Journal*, September 23, 2013.

5. David Román and Christopher Bjork, "Bill Gates Buys Stake in Spanish Construction Company FCC," *Wall Street Journal*, October 22, 2013.

6. Christopher Bjork and Richard Boudreaux, "Private-Equity Firm H.I.G. to Buy Spanish Real-Estate Assets," *Wall Street Journal*, August 6, 2013.

7. PwC and ULI, *Emerging Trends Europe 2013*, 40.

CHAPTER SEVEN

Be Passionate about the Business

ACROSS EVERY INDUSTRY, ONE TRAIT distinguishes those who succeed from those who never really give themselves a chance—passion. Deeply encoded in the DNA of business leaders and entrepreneurs, passion is what gets them up in the morning and why they work long days and often well into the night.

Nowhere does passion play a greater role as a motivator than in real estate. Even among the most stoic leaders, it is impossible to be in this business without absolutely loving it. Two very different individuals—British property investor Nicholas "Nick" Leslau and Patrick Kanters, managing director, global real estate and infrastructure, for APG Asset Management—exhibit their passion for the business in their own ways.

Nerve and Patience: Nick Leslau

Nicholas "Nick" Leslau has been chairman and chief executive of Prestbury Investment Holdings since it was founded in October 2000. Before that, he was named non-executive chairman of Prestbury Group Plc in December 1997 and was appointed group chairman and chief executive of Prestbury Group in January 1998. He is also founder of Max Property Group, the property manager for Prestbury Investment Holdings; Max Property is listed on the AIM, the London

Stock Exchange's platform for smaller, growing companies. Prestbury's £3 billion property portfolio includes theme parks, hotels, health care facilities, and other conventional properties.

Previously, Leslau was chief executive of Burford Holdings plc for about ten years, until his resignation from its board in 1997. He has served on the boards of many public and private companies and is a member of the Bank of England Property Forum. He is a chartered surveyor.

Leslau, chairman and chief executive of Prestbury Investment Holdings and founder of the Max Property Group, is known by other titles in the press, such as "property millionaire" and "property tycoon," and as one of Britain's wealthiest property entrepreneurs (his personal net worth has been pegged at about £200 million). He is also known for being part owner of the Saracens rugby team (which he calls "a very expensive, passionate hobby") and for amassing an extensive collection of sports memorabilia, such as a cricket bat signed by W.G. Grace, a 19th-century cricket player thought to be the greatest of all time. In real estate development and investment, he is a true leader.

In interviews for this book, Leslau shows a bit of the brash and outspoken personality for which he is known. However, he projects far more of his savvy for running a diverse portfolio, almost all of it in the United Kingdom, ranging from Travelodge hotels and health care properties to entertainment properties such as Madame Tussauds, the iconic wax museum of historical and popular figures.

Leslau is much less a developer and far more an investor, roles that call for two distinct yet complementary traits: nerve and patience. "You need huge [nerve]"—a toned-down synonym for the word he uses—"to be a developer, and the rewards are much bigger," Leslau says. "To be an investor, you need more patience . . . perhaps a little more calculating in terms of acting for the long term strategically."

With his drive, commitment, and passion, Leslau has been successful in real estate, not an easy business, particularly at the scale undertaken by any of the people featured in this book. With a strict focus on the fundamentals, Leslau has managed the upswings and downturns of real estate cycles for more than 30 years. In fact, he has been credited with calling the top of the property market at the end of 2006. He is also credited with calling the top of the market in 1988, when his firm went entirely to net cash—a move that led to a year of criticism, followed by many more years of applause.

The challenges in the real estate field, though considerable, are not without appeal, as any of those profiled in this book would attest. For one thing, there is something special about real estate—as tangible an asset as one might imagine, whether it is a restored historic building in London or a new shopping center in a secondary city. As Leslau has said: "If you don't have a go, if you have no skin in the game, you're never going to win or lose."[1]

Without passion for the real estate industry, it is difficult if not impossible to maintain one's motivation through the inevitable ups and downs of building a business. Entrepreneurship of any sort is not for the faint of heart. Passion provides sustenance when nearly all else fails. But passion must be coupled with hard work in order for a person to realize the vision and execute the plan.

The Milkman's Apprentice

Leslau developed a passion for business at an early age, starting with the most basic of motivations—he needed money. He describes his early years with aplomb: the son of a father who owned a small jewelry shop in "not a particularly nice part of north London." His parents divorced when he was a boy, and money was tight. Fortunately, he had a wealthy grandfather on his mother's side who paid the tuition for Leslau and his brothers to attend private school (most notably, Mill Hill School in London), though they continued to live in a very modest house. "I have memories of deciding that I didn't like the fact that all my friends had new soccer boots or cricket bats and mine were all from the secondhand shop and the thrift shop," Leslau says. "They all got picked up in Rolls Royces and Jaguars and I would go on the bus."

Making money became the obvious way to fill that void. An early job was helping the milkman make his rounds, for which Leslau was paid 50 pence a week. Later he resold umbrellas in a market stall. One of his most formative experiences, when he was 18 or so, was a job at a late-night convenience store. When the owner popped in one day and asked young Leslau his thoughts on how the store was run, he listed a dozen possible improvements. Although Leslau, by his own admission, "knew nothing about anything" at the time, when the owner gave him permission to implement his ideas, he did. Within six weeks, sales improved by 30 percent.

"In those two months, the world changed for me," Leslau says. "Suddenly I thought, 'Hey, I can do this.'" (Coincidentally, a customer at the store was financier and Mill Hill alum Nigel Wray, with whom he would later partner.) Leslau transformed from an eager store clerk to a passionate, entrepreneurial-minded businessman-in-the-making.

Equally important, Leslau in his early days developed another attribute—the willingness to work hard. "I was never scared of hard work because I liked making money," he says. As is the case with many successful entrepreneurs, Leslau learned early the importance of doing whatever it takes to get a job done.

Kanters discovered the same thing. "When there is a lot of hard work to do, when it becomes almost a 24-hour workday, you cannot be afraid to roll up your sleeves every now and then," he says.

Directing intense efforts toward a specific goal also ignites one's passion. Then, no matter how difficult, the endeavor becomes highly motivating and a reason to put forth one's best.

Entrepreneurial Ventures

Leslau studied German at Warwick University, then switched to a degree in estate management at what is now London South Bank University (previously South Bank Polytechnic), where he found his niche. In 1982, he joined Burford Group's fledgling property division worth €200,000.

While at Burford, Leslau became a qualified chartered surveyor and was made junior partner in 1983. Burford went public in 1986 at £8 million in valuation with Leslau as managing director—at 27, the youngest managing director of any publicly traded company in the United Kingdom. In 1987, Wray bought Burford for £56 million. The two joined forces, Leslau as chief executive and Wray as chairman. Together, they expanded Burford Group over the next ten years into a £1.2 billion-net-worth property company, delivering growth of 1,300 percent net asset value per share in the process.

Notable deals during that time were acquisitions along Oxford Street, one of Europe's busiest retail areas; the Trocadero Center in London's Piccadilly Circus, a historic location converted to entertainment and retail space; and the creation of Segaworld, a video game–themed entertainment center that, although promising, failed to live up to expectations. In an interview with the *Guardian*, Leslau said Segaworld's indoor theme park lacked sufficient personnel, and customers had to wait in long lines for rides. "It was a question of overanticipation and underdelivery," he added. However, Leslau emphasized that Segaworld was a "PR disaster, but not a financial disaster," adding, "You learn a lot from the ones that go wrong."[2]

New Opportunities

In 2008, Leslau was buying properties again, and that summer decided it was time to go to the public markets to raise money for Max Property Group, of which he is now a non-executive director. Max Property's initial public offering in early 2009 was the largest in Europe that year. The timing appeared fortuitous, with British property values having fallen by nearly 45 percent and indications that the decline was slowing. Seeing bargains to be had, Max Property went to the public market to raise money for fresh deals.[3]

In Leslau's view, the public market was the only way to raise discretionary money (funds invested by a professional manager on behalf of investors/clients). The alternative would have been nondiscretionary money, which Leslau saw as unworkable. "I have never operated with nondiscretionary money. It's tough enough doing deals when you can sign the check, let alone going to someone else to talk them through it and get their buy-in," he says.

Among the crowning achievements for Leslau has been his purchase in 2011 of the historic St. Katharine Docks near the Tower of London. When Leslau completed the £156 million deal, it was hailed in the press as "the greatest undertaking of his career"—a six-building parcel that he planned to refurbish and lease to financial services firms and other tenants. St. Katharine Docks had come on the market after former owners defaulted on a £170 million loan. Leslau bested other competitors for the historic and unique real estate development site. "It's very rare to get ten acres in central London for £330 per square foot,"[4] he said.

The site has 46,450 square meters of offices, restaurants, and shops surrounding the only marina in central London. At the time of the deal, it generated annual rent of £12.6 million, and had a 12 percent vacancy rate. Leslau's plan to reduce vacancies included property improvements and a broader tenant mix.[5]

Leslau has also made investments that are more defensive in nature—properties that are insulated somewhat from the cyclicity of real estate. For example, because he considers the health care sector to be defensive and profitable given the aging of the population, he has invested in hospitals, nursing homes, and other health care assets.

Leslau is drawn to opportunities that require the ability to act boldly. Yet he declares that he is no gambler. "For me it's like, if I really like a deal, I can't wait it out for months to see it possibly get cheaper and cheaper, because if the downside is well protected, then let's go for it," Leslau says. Such an action-oriented approach requires passion and the confidence that comes from having enjoyed victories and endured disappointments. Leslau sees this mode of conducting business as preferable to the alternative that can afflict some entrepreneurs—paralysis by analysis. For them, the problem is too much caution, which Leslau describes as "yeah, no, yeah, no, okay, we'll do it," or having too many choices, which he calls "we could do this, we could do that, and we're not making a decision at all."

"Business is about risk taking," he concludes. Protecting a portfolio of investments and/or developments is accomplished through constant stress-testing on the basis of worst-case scenarios. But failing to act on an opportunity is also a huge risk because it stymies growth and allows competitors to gain the upper hand.

"I do think our DNA gives us something that makes us more willing to put our foot forward and lead—going out and doing something—and taking people with you," Leslau says of successful real estate investors and developers. "The best entrepreneurs are the best salespeople. You've got to bring people with you."

A key factor in that genetic code of leadership is best defined by one decisive factor—passion.

A Passion for Real Estate: Patrick Kanters

Patrick Kanters is managing director, global real estate and infrastructure, at Netherlands-based APG Asset Management. APG handles asset management, administration, and communication for large and medium-sized pension funds in the public and private sectors.

Based in APG's Amsterdam office, Kanters is responsible for all the pension funds' real estate investments. These holdings are concentrated in securities of publicly traded real estate companies and selected private entities, funds, and co-investments in Europe, the Americas, and the Asia Pacific region.

Before joining APG, Kanters spent 11 years with ING Real Estate, a Netherlands-based firm that manages a variety of real estate investments around the world. Kanters is also a member of the board of Steen & Strom, the leading Scandinavian shopping center investor, operator, and developer. He has a master's degree in real estate, project management, and housing from the Delft University of Technology, and a postdoctoral degree in real estate from the University of Amsterdam.

"There was just something about real estate," says Kanters, recalling his early passion for the business. As a youth, Kanters tracked the housing market, poring over property listings in the newspaper, "which was probably not a normal habit for a kid who was only 14," he laughs.

Upon entering Delft University, Kanters started studying architecture, but after completing an apprenticeship, discovered it was not an ideal fit for him. Although the desire to be an architect did not last, he still collects architecture books. More interesting to him than the design process was the financial side of the industry, which led him to study real estate management and development.

Most interesting about Kanters's story is how he developed a passion for the business early on. Highly successful executives across all industries often develop an early interest in business or exhibit an entrepreneurial streak as a youth. In real estate investment, Kanters found his niche. Fortunately for him, he was also given key development opportunities early in his career that made a lasting impression, especially teaching him the importance of teamwork. He recalls a boss from ING who facilitated opportunities for team members to grow and gain experience. Later, when he became the boss leading the team, Kanters took it upon himself to create an environment in which people could work at the peak of their capabilities. "When team members flourish, they can perform at their maximum," he says. "That has everything to do with setting clear goals and creating an environment that promotes a very positive mind-set and being entrepreneurial."

When these factors come together, passion becomes contagious. People are not only happy to reap extrinsic rewards that come with making money, but they also find fulfillment in their work. "It is very much about creating team spirit and mobilizing others. This means not only people within your team, because if you want to get things done in the outside world, it is about mobilizing limited partners and general partners," he adds.

Bringing Out the Best in Others

Entrepreneurs are rarely known for being great coaches and teachers who want to devote time to developing their team members and transferring skills and knowledge to them. Business builders tend to be impatient and demanding; it is often seen as better for people who cannot keep up to get out of the way. Therefore, when a leader is passionate about building a business *and* developing others, it is an unusual and valued combination.

Kanters is an example of that rare breed of leader who has a true passion for mentoring and training others. "It is very hard work—listening a lot and giving space to people," Kanters says. Developing people in real estate often means working closely with them and going over the details of deals so they can learn by example and gain experience. In a business that demands a 24-hour workday, the added responsibility of team development is another significant commitment. Yet Kanters sees it as valuable work for a leader. Ultimately, devoting time and attention to both the team and the organization establishes a cultural value that yields dividends over time.

A Focus on the Core Business

Among the lessons to be imparted to the next generation of real estate leaders is the importance of discernment, particularly regarding potential opportunities, Kanters says. During the boom days before the 2008–2009 global financial crisis, he observes, some people were lulled into a sense of being "good at everything because everything was turning to gold." As a result, people tended to be generalists, developing little depth or expertise in certain areas. "They were greedy—wanting to do this and wanting to do that," he says.

Today, with the benefit of hindsight to view the devastating effects of the crisis, Kanters points out the problems that can arise when people venture outside their niche areas without sufficient experience or support. It is often a recipe that includes taking on too much risk, shouldering too much leverage, paying too much for assets, or a combination of the three.

When the downturn comes, these noncore activities are inevitably the first to become problematic.

Discerning Opportunities

With years of experience comes the ability to broaden one's horizons across sectors and geographies. When Kanters joined APG, he became head of real estate for Europe and the Asia Pacific region, taking on an increasingly global portfolio that includes listed and nonlisted investments, joint ventures, and co-investments. (Nonlisted investment vehicles are alternative investments that are generally more illiquid than investments in other assets, such as stocks and bonds.) APG's total investments are worth about €25 billion, across the Americas, Europe, and the Asia Pacific.

Kanters is also chairman of the European Association for Investors in Non-Listed Real Estate Vehicles (INREV), which is Europe's leading platform for sharing information on the nonlisted real estate industry. As part of INREV's leadership, Kanters has pressed for greater standardization, with uniform valuation methodologies to be used worldwide. Improved standardization and transparency, he believes, will be of great benefit to all players in the industry.

Kanters also has been a proponent of environmental sustainability, both in his work at APG and through INREV. One such initiative, the Global Real Estate Sustainability Benchmark, involves assessing the environmental and social performance of listed and nonlisted real estate investments. "Every fund manager and joint venture sponsor needs a proper sustainability policy today—both for short-term and long-term strategies," he has said. "We are way past the point that more sustainable real estate involves higher costs. Improving the level of sustainability of your investments actually increases their value. It will cost if you are not sustainable."[6]

Like other real estate companies, when APG looks at Europe, it takes a city-specific focus to capitalize on urbanization and growth trends— especially in London, Paris, Stockholm, and Oslo. "Europe is likely to be a prolonged low-growth environment, and parts of it do not have a rosy demographic outlook," Kanters says.

Capitalizing on changes in demographics, which tend to favor cities, means finding opportunities in specific niches, such as seniors' housing, midrange-price-point housing, and student housing. Sounding a theme similar to that of Alexander Otto on the need for bricks-and-mortar retail space despite the inroads of e-commerce, Kanters believes some shopping center formats will continue to be competitive. "We are in the process of optimizing our portfolio toward the larger-scale projects that prove to be a unique experience for people," he says. Properties that are in lower-growth environments will be "less forgiving" if developers focus on the wrong assets, he adds.

Among the opportunities APG has pursued are residential and retail assets in London, including an investment in the Westfield Stratford City shopping center in Stratford, which is owned by the Westfield Group and opened in September 2011. APG invested alongside Westfield Group as one of the few players large enough to take on such an integrated project that called for development of retail, residential, and leisure space.

Daring to Be Different

As both Leslau and Kanters observe, having passion allows one to move beyond missed opportunities and overcome mistakes rather than become limited by them. In any business, no one makes the right call all the time. With experience, though, comes the confidence to say yes at what appear to be opportune moments, as well as no when risk is too great or other factors simply do not add up.

At times this will mean being a bit of a contrarian—for example, buying when one is convinced there are bargains to be had even though others remain on the sidelines, and turning down deals when others are charging ahead. Whatever the strategy, one must have the conviction and passion to follow through. "Do not take half measures," Kanters says. "If you decide to go left, then go left, not somewhere near left, even if that means you are going in a different direction than other people. Dare to be different."

Taking the proverbial road less traveled in real estate also means not rushing. The objective is not to do as many deals in as short a time as possible, but to pursue solid opportunities, learn from the outcome (win or lose), and amass experience that can be put to good use the next time. Kanters also explains the importance in real estate of social skills — networking and developing relationships with others. In order to develop a reputation for being authentic, a person must take the time to nurture such connections.

Asked what he would say to the next generation of real estate leaders, Kanters offers this advice: "Take your time in your career. Enjoy the things you are doing. Don't just strive to reach another goal. If you enjoy what you do, then you are going to be good at it." Then, passion leads to the real payoff.

Building Blocks of Leadership

➤ Real estate leaders must act boldly when opportunities present themselves, but always with an eye toward risk containment. Ensuring that the downside is well protected is a prerequisite for taking action. Such boldness requires passion and confidence, which can only be developed with experience, including both victories and disappointments. Lessons learned help pave the way to success.

➤ Discernment is an essential skill for real estate leaders, who must proceed with extreme caution when venturing outside their niches of expertise. Going into what looks like a promising new area or pursuing an unfamiliar opportunity without sufficient support or experience may lead to too much risk exposure, overleverage, or paying too much for assets. The devastation of the 2008–2009 financial crisis serves as a painful reminder of what can happen when noncore investments or developments become problematic.

Notes

1. Julia Kollewe, "Secret Millionaire Nick Leslau Buys St. Katharine Docks," *Guardian*, June 28, 2011.

2. Ibid.

3. Deal Book, "British Real Estate Investors Add Life to I.P.O. Market," *New York Times*, June 12, 2009, http://dealbook.nytimes.com/2009/06/12/uk-real-estate-investors-add-life-to-ipo-market/?_r=0.

4. Kollewe, "Secret Millionaire Nick Leslau."

5. Ibid.

6. INREV, "Member Profiles: Patrick Kanters," *IQ*, June 2012, www.inrev.org/news/iq-magazine/issue-11-june-2012/1169-patrick-kanters.

CHAPTER EIGHT

Pursue Lifelong Learning

ARE LEADERS BORN, OR ARE THEY MADE? A study of leadership inevitably leads to the conclusion that it is both. Although some qualities are inborn and some people qualify as "natural leaders," *all* leadership is enhanced by lifelong learning, starting with experiences early in one's career. Over time, someone who is capable becomes highly competent, but only with continuous learning.

Exemplifying lifelong learning is Serge Fautré, chief executive officer of AG Real Estate, a unit of Ageas of Belgium. With a long career in the real estate industry, he has firsthand knowledge of what it takes to lead with integrity and authenticity.

An Investment in Education: Serge Fautré

Serge Fautré is chief executive officer of AG Real Estate, the real estate unit of Belgian insurer Ageas. He joined AG in 2012 after ten years as CEO and managing director of Cofinimmo S.A., starting in 2002.

Previously, Fautré was finance director of the internet business unit and director of the treasury and finance group at Belgacom, the largest telecommunications company in Belgium. From 1994 to 1999, he was head of the Belgian investment banking department at JPMorgan, and from 1992 to 1994 headed the corporate finance department in the Glaverbel Group. Fautré also worked at

Citibank, first in Brussels, where he was responsible for all transactions related to financial engineering and capital markets, and then in London. He began his professional career in New York at J. Henri Schroder Bank and Trust Company.

Fautré currently is vice chairman of Interparking S.A. and vice chairman and a non-executive director of Ascencio. He holds a master of business administration degree (1983) and an undergraduate degree in economics from the University of Chicago.

Growing up in Belgium, Fautré remembers what his mother called "the Harvard envelope," which contained money she carefully saved for years. It was a significant commitment and sacrifice; his parents divorced when Fautré was young, and his mother had to support herself and her children, as well as her mother. In addition to the francs tucked away in the envelope every week, Fautré's mother made another investment: sending him at a very young age to a private tutor to learn English because there were no language classes at his primary school. "I have been raised and educated with a certain ambition to get an international education. That was always part of my background," Fautré recalls.

Although the envelope was for Harvard, Fautré ended up attending (with a full scholarship) the University of Chicago, another very highly regarded institution, and received his MBA there in 1983. (He did, however, spend six weeks as a college-bound student at the Harvard Summer School to improve his English. Recently, when a friend asked for advice to prepare his son for college, Fautré immediately suggested the Harvard program in order to give the young man a taste of campus life and to ignite his ambition.)

After graduate school, Fautré was hired by J. Henri Schroder Bank and Trust Company in New York, which provided him with a foundation in finance that would later distinguish his career. For any CEO, and especially one in real estate, strong training in finance is essential, especially in-depth knowledge of analyzing and financing investments. "I think having a financial foundation is useful because a lot of real estate activity has to do with the financial markets—maybe even more than if someone were running a company in another industry," Fautré says.

Financial knowledge also helps in another aspect of real estate, particularly for firms that are publicly held and therefore must communicate with investors and other stakeholders. "A leader also needs to know how to communicate to the financial markets, which is as important as understanding the financial markets themselves," Fautré says.

Over the years, his teachers, mentors, and role models have been as varied as the lessons they taught: one might impart technical skills while another provided insights into being a good leader. All were essential to his education in real estate and leadership. "In each organization, I found somebody who was willing to spend time with me and help me," he says.

Fautré counts among his mentors his stepfather (his mother remarried when he was young), whom he describes as supportive, and later his father-in-law, who had a career in finance. In the professional world, his education has been a bit unorthodox at times but nonetheless highly effective. For example, when he moved back to Brussels in 1985 to work for Citibank, instead of attending the company's formal training sessions, for nine months he spent several hours a day being mentored by his manager. "He said he wanted to teach me everything he knew," Fautré recalls. Although he struggled at first to keep up with his boss, Fautré was committed to deepening his financial knowledge. "After a while, I started understanding."

Building on his expertise in finance and investment, Fautré became head of the Belgian investment banking department at JPMorgan, a position he held from 1994 to 1999. That job took him to London, where he worked with many Europeans and Americans, absorbing a cross-cultural mix of attitudes and perspectives that proved highly educational. "Cross-cultural exchanges can be very enriching," Fautré says. "For example, the Americans can teach us [Europeans] to be proud of our successes. The U.S. is proud of what it is; Europeans are probably not proud enough of what they are. It's a balance: Europe has got to learn from the U.S., the U.S. from Asia, and Asia from Europe."

In 2002, Fautré joined Cofinimmo, a leading real estate investment manager in Belgium listed on Euronext Brussels. With a strong presence in the European market, it holds a portfolio worth more than €3 billion and properties in Belgium, France, and the Netherlands. For a leader with a global mind-set and a cross-cultural perspective, running a pan-European operation was a logical next step.

At the time, though, Fautré was only 40 and considered by most to be young for a CEO. Fortunately, he had an influential mentor, Cofinimmo chairman André Dirckx (formerly of Generale Bank), who was his sounding board for the next ten years. This experience illustrates that even when an executive reaches the top of the organization, learning can and must continue.

The relationship was particularly important during the financial crisis of 2008–2009. "It was an incredible comfort to have a chairman of the board tell me, 'Listen: first, you are not responsible for the financial storms. You are only responsible for weathering the storms—for making sure we stay afloat and that we don't sink. That is a lot more important,'" Fautré recalls. "It was wonderful advice because when you are in charge, you tend to take the negative things personally."

Fautré spent a decade with Cofinimmo, a long time for a CEO to serve and a testament to his contribution to the organization. He is credited with leading a diversification drive, acquiring nursing homes, and participating in public/private partnerships for assets such as prisons and fire stations. In 2007, Fautré bought most of InBev NV's Belgian and Dutch pubs. (InBev is a Belgian-Brazilian multinational beverage company.) Such moves reduced Cofinimmo's exposure to the Belgian office market, which had been its major holding but now accounts for less than half its portfolio. More than 20 percent of its investments today are outside Belgium, particularly in France.[1]

In early 2012, Fautré's appointment as CEO of AG Real Estate was announced. AG Real Estate is active in real estate development, asset management, and property management, with holdings that include Interparking, which operates car parking facilities in Europe. The move answered what the press had hailed as "one of the biggest [succession] questions in

the Belgian real estate world," raised when preceding CEO Alain Devos
announced his intention to step down. Devos called his successor's appointment "both logical and natural," adding that the "diversity and wide
range of activities within AG Real Estate will give [Fautré] the opportunity
to make good use of all his skills in the most varied domains of real estate."[2]

Communicating the Message

Fautré brought to his new position at AG Real Estate a wealth of experience in real estate and finance, as well as leadership lessons he learned
along the way. Among the most important of those was how to build and
motivate a team. "There are obviously differences among leaders—some
are more charismatic, for example—but the ability to motivate a team is
fundamental to staying power as a leader," he says. "That ability to motivate has a lot to do with the ability to instill trust among the people in the
organization—and also with people outside the organization."

Fautré uses the example of the Steve Jobs, who was the undisputed
face of Apple. Yet even this iconic leader was not solely responsible for
execution of the strategy. "The success of Steve Jobs was being able to communicate with and motivate the team," he says.

His point is well taken: CEOs can be great visionaries, but success for
an organization ultimately rests in a team that can execute a strategy. As a
company gets bigger, it must have more decision makers and influencers.
The leader cannot be the only one in charge. "You can be visionary, but
you are nothing if you are not developing your team," Fautré says. "If you
don't, you are probably going to be a short-term leader."

Learning from the Mistakes of Others

An important element in the education of any leader is learning from the
mistakes made by others, particularly those who are highly accomplished. No
matter how competent a leader may be, no one is infallible. This in itself is a
powerful lesson. "First, they've got to admit that to themselves," Fautré says.

Effective leaders also have the self-confidence to share the lessons
learned from their setbacks and mistakes. In fact, valued mentors will readily

share not only the secrets of success behind their victories, but also the details of their mistakes so that others can benefit from them. Perhaps a strategy was ill-timed or an opportunity did not turn out as planned. Learning from the mistakes of others may very well prevent a similar occurrence in one's own career.

One common mistake among executives, Fautré observes, is a lack of self-awareness and humility. These traits, especially, allow a leader to connect authentically with others and thus avoid another common mistake among executives—isolation. "They lose a sense of reality," Fautré continues. "They lose perspective. They take themselves too seriously. They believe they are above all the rest." Fautré sounds a warning as he gives sage advice to the next generation of leaders, drawing from his own discipline as well as the mistakes made by others: "Speak with people. Don't isolate yourself. Keep your university friends and your high school friends. Listen to your spouse."

Forgetting where you came from is a dangerous trap embedded in the territory of the C-suite. Far too often when people reach a certain level, they change—and usually not in a positive way. Job titles and the perquisites of the position define them to the exclusion of all else. Personal relationships, particularly those that are long term, are the best antidote: you cannot forget where you came from. "My wife very regularly tells me, 'Remember, if some people are nice to you, don't believe it is because of you. It is because of your success, image, etc.' So you have to remain very modest. Some are better able to do that than others. But humility needs to stay constant," he adds.

Keeping a Balanced Perspective

Even when a leader attains a high degree of success, unmet goals and unfulfilled ambitions will remain. Some will be outright disappointments— for example, a dream job that never comes to fruition. Others will be what Fautré calls "realities"; for example, he has not yet managed a global enterprise. He acknowledges it, but does not dwell on what he did not accomplish. "I am too much a positive thinker to focus on disappointments. When I look at the overall picture, it is one I enjoy very much."

Fautré is confident that his career has progressed in a way that best suited him. Indeed, there are many possible paths to take; success comes from following the one that is most authentic. For instance, Fautré does not see himself as an entrepreneur, which he defines as someone able to build a company from scratch. "That's not really in my genes," he says. "I am more of a manager than an entrepreneur."

Such self-acceptance stems from knowing one's strengths and weaknesses, likes and dislikes. For Fautré, this has been a lesson well learned and well lived, which enhances his leadership.

Building Blocks of Leadership

➤ Mentors and advisers are not only essential for those who are starting out, but also for more senior executives, who benefit from candid advice and feedback. Early on, the mentor/mentored relationship is grounded in formative experiences—the former providing exposure and content to the latter. Later, relationships become more peer-to-peer, with the mentor serving as a sounding board.

➤ Self-knowledge is an essential leadership trait. Knowing oneself—both strengths and weaknesses—develops self-confidence, which ultimately enhances competence. With self-awareness comes the ability to admit one's mistakes and to share the lessons learned with the team. Humility triggers reflection, but not at the cost of owning one's successes, which is also important. In the end, it is all about balance.

Notes

1. Andrew Clapham, "Cofinimmo Chief Fautré Resigns to Head Ageas Real-Estate Unit," Bloomberg News, March 23, 2012, www.bloomberg.com/news/2012-03-23/cofinimmo-chief-fautre-resigns-to-head-ageas-real-estate-unit.html.

2. Pro-RealEstate.be, "Serge Fautré to Take Over at AG Real Estate," March 22, 2012, www.pro-realestate.be/news-view.asp?ID=74706&L=uk&ccc=&rrr=&chann el=&rubr=&V=title&TXT=Serge%20Fautr%E9%20to%20take%20over%20at%20 AG%20Real%20Estate.

CHAPTER NINE

Build and Preserve
a Legacy

IN ANY BUSINESS OR INDUSTRY, A SELECT GROUP of leaders exists whose focus extends beyond their own term at the helm. They readily acknowledge the contributions of those who came before them and are equally cognizant of those who will follow. Although they are the beneficiaries of the foundation that was laid by others, they are responsible for what now occurs on their watch. It is up to them to leave the organization healthier and in better shape than what they inherited so that others might take the enterprise even further. This is the essence of building and preserving a legacy.

In the bricks-and-mortar business of real estate, and especially in European real estate that spans centuries, legacy is found, literally, in the buildings preserved and refurbished, neighborhoods revitalized, and properties developed. Although some buildings are closely associated with a person (in the United States, the hotels and towers bearing the name "Trump" are an obvious example), true leaders do not seek to erect a monument to themselves. Rather, they act more as stewards, entrusted with the well-being of an organization during a specific time and under specific circumstances.

Though these leaders undertake property investment, development, and management as a business that generates a profit, they do not act for that reason alone. A legacy is established by building something that truly matters, for the benefit of a variety of stakeholders—investors, customers/tenants, employees, and the residents of a particular city or neighborhood. Sir John Ritlbat is one of those investor/developers.

A Walk to Remember: Sir John Ritblat

Sir John Ritblat is the retired chairman and honorary president of the British Land Company PLC. Formerly, he was CEO and chairman of the company, which he acquired in 1970. Today, he is chairman of Delancey, a family-owned real estate advisory company, and has served as non-executive chairman and director of Colliers CRE plc.

Earlier in his career, Ritblat was managing director of Union Property, and was cofounder of Conrad Ritblat & Company, of which he was senior partner and chairman.

Ritblat is the chairman and honorary fellow and a member of the board of governors of the London Business School. He was a member of the board of the British Library, which features the Sir John Ritblat Treasures Gallery, housing a collection of illuminated manuscripts and other valuable documents. He is a vice president of the Royal Institution of Great Britain and was a member of its council. He is president of the British Ski & Snowboard Federation. He is chairman of the Wallace Collection (a British art museum) and an honorary trustee and honorary Fellow of the Royal Academy of Music (FRAM), where he was a governor and deputy chairman from 1998 to 2012. He has been a trustee of International Students House since 1970, as well as a member of the Council of Governors since 2003 and vice chairman since 2007. He is a Fellow of the Royal Institution of Chartered Surveyors (FRICS), an honorary Fellow of the Royal Institute of British Architects (FRIBA), a Companion of the Chartered Management Institute (CCMI), and a life Fellow of the Royal Society of Arts (FRSA). He has several honorary degrees.

Ritblat was deputy chairman of the Hall School in Hampstead from 1997 to 2003 and is now a fellow of Dulwich College, where he was a governor from 2003 to 2009 and where he remains a consultant to the governing body.

In the years following World War II, young John Ritblat took a walk through the streets of London with his uncle, who at the time was involved in real estate development in the city's West End. Today, the West End is a fashionable, bustling area of galleries, restaurants, and stores. Then, circa 1950, it was a far different scene. "When we walked around, it was in a terrible state," Ritblat recalls. "Every other building was an empty site that had been bombed. My uncle very wisely said to me, 'We're not going to leave things like this. Britain will rebuild, and there will be a great opportunity to revitalize the U.K.'"

For young John, his uncle's words were not only inspiring, but also extremely practical. In those few words, Ritblat received the direction for his professional life. Today, he is Sir John Ritblat, knighted in 2006 in recognition of his philanthropy in the arts. Called the "grand old man of British property,"[1] he retired in 2006 as chairman of the British Land Company and now holds the title of honorary president. He spent 36 years at the top of the FTSE 100 company, an incredibly long time for any executive, with a tenure that has encompassed some of the industry's most prominent booms and busts.

Ritblat's legacy is impressive. He bought British Land from Jim Slater in 1970 for £1 million; by the time he retired, the company, founded in 1856, was worth almost £7 billion. According to its 2008 annual report, British Land then managed a portfolio of commercial property worth more than £20 billion. But there are no monuments to Ritblat: you will not find a "Ritblat Tower or Ritblat Mall."[2] But there have been signature investments and developments during Ritblat's long career. Among the most notable is Broadgate, a 14-hectare premier office estate in the heart of London—16 separate office buildings, alongside retail and leisure properties. The 164-meter Broadgate Tower is one of London's tallest buildings.

Broadgate was wholly owned by British Land from 2003 to 2009, when it sold 50 percent of the property to the Blackstone Group. In late 2013, Blackstone sold its Broadgate stake to GIC, the Singapore sovereign wealth fund, for about £1.7 billion.

Much of what Ritblat has accomplished over his long and successful career can be traced back to those early walks around London with his uncle, when he learned the importance of revitalization as both business opportunity and civic contribution. In the days immediately following the war, building licenses were issued only for priority construction, particularly residential development. Over time, though, other kinds of development were badly needed as life returned to normal.

In the early 1950s, Ritblat was articled (akin to an apprenticeship) to Edward Erdman, a prominent, longtime London property agent. To this day, Ritblat considers Erdman's mentorship to have been extremely important to his career. For young Ritblat, it was total immersion: he was concurrently attending the College of Estate Management at London University, learning the business, and being exposed to "some very major transactions with some of the best investors, institutions, and developers of all time."

In the late 1950s, Ritblat and a partner, Neville Conrad, founded Conrad Ritblat & Co., which specialized in retail and office properties. "We were—how can I put it?—dormant stakeholders," he recalls. "We just held some properties for investment. One was able to finance very easily in those days. . . . Times were very good [economically] through the 1950s and the beginning of the 1960s. And so we gradually started doing commercial development."

Things were so good at this first company that Ritblat almost stopped his career right there. "I nearly stopped before I started," he told the *Telegraph.* "I was in a position to do so. I had the Conrad Ritblat practice and some investments. I thought seriously of retirement."[3]

Then opportunity knocked. Ritblat was asked by Maxwell Joseph to help sort out some problems at a small, public real estate company called Union Property. As part of the deal, Ritblat added some of his own properties to the mix and became managing director. Then, in 1970, Union Property took over British Land and adopted its name. Over the course of the next several decades, Ritblat built British Land into one of Britain's top real estate firms—but not without facing his share of challenges as the industry went through a severe contraction.

Severe Challenges and Lessons Learned

The property crash of 1973 to 1975 was a real test for Ritblat and his contemporaries in British real estate investment and development. But unlike so many others, Ritblat survived. The story often told about him at the time has the soft patina of legend—how he candidly told his bankers that he was in far worse shape than they had thought, and how he acquired industrial businesses to generate cash flow. In short, he did whatever he had to do to keep the business afloat.

"You have to make mistakes because mistakes are what create experience," Ritblat says. "That's what I learned after the very difficult times in the early '70s." Labeling those times "difficult" is an understatement: the 1970s saw a steep decline in the stock market, interest rates soaring over 15 percent, and inflation that in Britain reached about 30 percent. No wonder Ritblat considers the 1970s crisis even more severe than the global economic shock of 2008–2009.

For Ritblat, the greatest challenge of the 1970s came in 1977, when British Land had two large loan redemptions due—one for £10 million and one for £15 million, which at the time were "enormous," he says—and the company could not refinance them because banks refused to lend. Instead, Ritblat and two financiers used their own money. To say it ended well is to put it mildly: the British Land stock, which had dipped to a few pence per share, recovered and profits were made all around.

"What I learned is this: you need to have reserves for a rainy day," Ritblat says. "There is no substitute for the long term."

Having witnessed the professional demise of so many of his contemporaries in real estate in the 1970s and in subsequent severe downturns, Ritblat affirms the importance of what he calls being financially aware. "Indeed, half of our business has to do with money, and the other half is real estate," he says. "I always paid a great deal of attention to the way in which my affairs were funded."

Financial prudence does not preclude being entrepreneurial or even opportunistic. However, one must always keep in mind that profits (and legacies) are made over the long term. Success requires the right priorities. "I used to say to my people, 'Money first, timing second, and deal third,'" Ritblat says.

Unquestionably, fiscal discipline is part of Ritblat's legacy, particularly in his role as financier and dealmaker/investor. Like other leaders profiled in this book, he has demonstrated the ability to look beyond the enticement of the short term and execute investment and development strategies that make the most sense through the cycles. Moreover, he possesses the courage and ability to anticipate, read, and react to changes in the cycles. For example, after building up a portfolio during the boom years of the 1980s, he began selling off properties late in that decade before the next slump occurred. What looks like farsightedness was actually the result of having been through a severe downturn before. Seeing the inflated levels of property values in the late 1980s and determining them to be unsustainable, Ritblat reined in his risk by reducing exposure and taking profits.

Selling before the slump also positioned British Land to buy during the recovery in the 1990s at bargain prices. Its purchase of an initial stake and then total ownership of Broadgate (before subsequent sale of half its stake) is an example of nabbing choice assets at the right price. Broadgate in many ways is the epitome of Ritblat's legacy in London real estate, even though development there continues long after his retirement. What matters most was not that Ritblat was there for the crowning glory, but that he was the one who created the opportunity for success.

Leadership and Legacy

Over his career, Ritblat has endured booms and busts, cycles, and reces-
sions. He has built a company into a "megalith"[4] and endured the scrutiny
of analysts and hedge fund managers who, from time to time, called for
British Land to be restructured. But he did not step down from the helm
until he was ready—the end of 2006—bringing to a close more than three-
and-a-half decades at the top of the organization, and with the shares and
net assets at all-time highs. His decision to retire at a time of his choosing,
rather than one dictated by others, reflects his independent nature.

The events marking his retirement provided a fitting send-off for
Ritblat that honored his legacy. At British Land's 2006 annual meeting,
shareholders gave Ritblat a standing ovation. At retirement ceremonies, he
handed out gold sovereign coins to long-serving employees—one coin for
each year of service (450 in all).[5]

Life after British Land remains busy for Ritblat, with many philan-
thropic endeavors, as well as the role as chairman of the advisory board of
family-owned Delancey, a specialist real estate investment and advisory
company; Ritblat's son James is the chief executive. In a 2008 interview, the
younger Ritblat said of working with his father, "You can't buy experience or
knowledge like that. He is here every day. He enjoys the life and the work,
and I think the people we have here value his presence and experience
hugely."[6] After the elder Ritblat joined Delancey's board in 2007, the company began withdrawing from the property market—before the worst of the
downturn.[7] Another son, Nick, a former director of British Land, has been
active in his own ventures and also headed the British Property Federation.

Looking back on his career, Ritblat pondered the timeless attributes
that contribute to leadership success. "You've got to be sufficiently confident to be a self-starter," he says. "That is something, I guess, you can be
trained for. But if you're fortunate, it is an innate aptitude and quality that
have been born in you. There is no substitute for learning your trade, but
if you can couple that with some innate abilities, so much the better. You

need drive and initiative—those are fundamental elements. But everything has to be predicated on understanding what you're doing."

Ritblat equates understanding with having "certain gifts of discernment," which, once again, combine in-born talent with life experience. Discernment applies to such strengths as being a good judge of character, particularly when it comes to selecting partners and recruiting and hiring associates. With discernment comes the confidence in one's team that facilitates delegating responsibilities—provided that a leader is smart enough to take that vital step. "I've seen it time and again—people who ought to be more successful fail to delegate and entrust responsibility to others," he says.

Reflecting on his own leadership and legacy, Ritblat considers himself fortunate to have worked with exceptional people in various capacities, including board members at British Land and at the various groups and organizations with which he has been involved. "I spent a great deal of time on a personal basis with many of them, so I knew their families well and all about their children," he says.

"I generally try to find people about whom I have previous knowledge, so I have some likelihood of making a sound judgment," he adds. "In fact, throughout my life, I have almost always recruited people with whom I had some business relationship or commercial activity. All in all, my key people were those with whom I have previous experiences. . . . Once again, there is absolutely no substitute for brains, allied with energy and commercial instinct."

His leadership legacy is enhanced by his work with so many distinguished directors over the years. "They were always people who had a lot to offer," Ritblat says. Key attributes for board members, he says, are being "brainy, courageous, and independent."

Ritblat also notes with pride that he was able to retain a large number of exceptionally loyal and talented people at British Land. "It think that was crucial, and it also gave me great satisfaction," he says. "We had the best pension [plans] you could have, and always noncontributory. We felt that if people were devoting themselves to company activities, then the quid pro quo was to ensure their health and well-being. That was a very, very important issue."

The Lasting Legacy

Another component of his leadership legacy is philanthropy, which has been both a corporate and personal value for Ritblat—and one he shares with many well-established leaders. In a spirit of giving back or of having a sense of obligation toward the communities in which they do business, many leaders undertake social, community, and/or cultural projects that benefit others.

Ritblat's activities have been varied, ranging from building art collections and supporting the arts to sponsoring exhibitions at the Tate Modern or National Gallery and performances at the Royal Opera. He even sponsors sporting events. One of his passions is skiing, and he served as president of the British Ski Federation and has been the principal sponsor of the British Alpine Ski Championships for more than 35 years. He also plays and sponsors tournaments in "real tennis" (also known as court tennis) and squash, and was vice president of the Tennis & Racquets Association. In addition, Ritblat has had a long association with the London Business School and chaired its board of governors. He also endowed the Science Media Centre at the Royal Institution of Great Britain.

Of all these activities, what Ritblat is perhaps best known for are his contributions to the British Library and the Wallace Collection, a national fine-arts museum in London. Both institutions have galleries named for him. During the presentation to Ritblat of an honorary degree of doctor of letters from the University of Buckingham, he was lauded as "an entrepreneur who is not only a figure of vision and accomplishment in business and public life, but who is also a man with a taste and passion for the arts."[8]

Passion for the arts has translated into enhancing the cultural treasures of his country through the British Library, where his £1 million endowment has made the Sir John Ritblat Treasures Gallery possible.

Here, priceless documents are displayed—medieval maps, a Gutenberg Bible from 1455, a first-folio edition of Shakespeare's works from 1623, Lewis Carroll's *Alice in Wonderland* with drawings by the author—as well as sketches by Da Vinci, musical scores by Bach and Mozart, Beethoven's tuning fork, John Lennon and Paul McCartney's handwritten lyrics to "A Hard Day's Night," and the Magna Carta, a singular historical record of rights granted by King John in 1215. For Ritblat, who has a deep interest in antiquarian books, the British Library provided a natural connection.

Moreover, preserving the treasures of the past as a legacy for the generations to come is a fitting avocation for Ritblat, whose personal and professional history has coincided with much of London's postwar property development. From the time he was articled as a 16-year-old until his retirement at age 70, Ritblat has witnessed, and in many cases participated in, notable commercial developments in London.

"It was a very special time," Ritblat says of those early days in the 1950s and 1960s. "The city and the West End were rather a closely woven community at the top." Doing business then put him in contact with many of the great leaders in business, such as Jack Cotton, who dominated postwar property development, and Sir Maxwell Joseph, founder of the Grand Metropolitan plc, a large British hotel group.

Now, Ritblat's name is on the list of influential people who have left their mark on the industry. "He is one of the great investors and has taught everyone in the industry a great deal,"[9] Stuart Lipton, himself a well-known developer, told the *Observer*.

The legacy Ritblat leaves is not only as a property developer, but also as a financier—recalling his own words focusing on the importance of financing to the business.

A true legacy is built by and through contributions to something greater than oneself. Although success and the financial fruits thereof are the basis for many a legacy, meaning is derived from lasting impact. Across the real estate industry, important legacies have been created and left by

leaders who have demonstrated the personal qualities and business acumen
that are essential to longevity in a highly cyclical and challenging industry.

By word and example, the European real estate leaders featured in
this book have paved the way to success for the next generation—provided
these younger investors and developers have the discipline and awareness
to follow in the footsteps of those who have survived the downturns (some
brutal) and capitalized on the upturns. This is the lasting legacy that will
define European real estate through its next phase and beyond.

Building Blocks of Leadership

➢   To be sure, real estate executives want to make a profit. But that is
not the only thing that motivates them. Often, they are guided by a bigger
vision and a deeper purpose that go well beyond today's business opportunities: they seek to build, preserve, and pass on a legacy. Building a legacy is
not about constructing monuments (real or figurative) to satisfy one's ego.
Rather, it involves ensuring that one's leadership truly makes a difference
for the organization and for the many stakeholders affected—employees,
customers/tenants, community residents, and others. What is built today
will have an impact that lasts well beyond the leadership of any one individual. With an eye toward leaving a legacy, leaders can weigh the impact of
their actions to ensure they are doing the right things for the right reasons.

➢   A legacy may be rooted in one's professional life and accomplishments,
but it often transcends the business arena. Leaders who have truly made
it—who have reached a level of achievement and reaped the resulting
financial rewards—often seek ways to make a difference for others. The
motivation may be to give back to a particular community or to champion
a particular passion, such as the arts or education. Whatever the endeavor,
philanthropy extends the reach of leadership through the contribution of
one's talent as well as treasure to organizations and causes. This is leadership that truly makes a difference that cannot be measured by a profit-and-
loss statement alone.

Notes

1. *Telegraph*, "Business Profile: Ritblat Casts Off from British Land," July 16, 2006, www.telegraph.co.uk/finance/2943451/Business-profile-Ritblat-casts-off-from-British-Land.html.

2. Ibid.

3. Ibid.

4. Heather Cannon, "The Charmer Who Built a Property Megalith," *Observer*, July 15, 2006, www.theguardian.com/business/2006/jul/16/theobserver.observerbusiness3.

5. *Telegraph*, "Business Profile: Riblat."

6. Jonathan Russell, "Cash is King . . . and Delancey's Got Plenty," *Telegraph*, March 29, 2008, www.telegraph.co.uk/finance/newsbysector/constructionandproperty/2787154/Cash-is-king...-and-Delanceys-got-plenty.html.

7. Ibid.

8. University of Buckingham Professor John Clarke, "Presentation speech for John Ritblat for the honorary degree of Doctor of Letters of the University *honoris causa*," June 6, 2013, www.buckingham.ac.uk/wp-content/uploads/2013/06/Sir-John-Riblat.pdf.

9. Cannon, "The Charmer."

CHAPTER TEN

What Differentiates the European Real Estate Leader?

THE RESEARCH FOR THIS BOOK YIELDED some unexpected insights about European real estate leadership. The most successful senior executives share three foundational attributes:

➤ they are instinctual;

➤ they have an appreciation for culture and complexity; and

➤ they manage for the long term.

These traits speak to value creation in European real estate and perseverance through the inevitable cycles of boom and bust, including the most recent severe downturn and recovery.

Moreover, these traits are not universally common among real estate leaders in other parts of the world. These leadership characteristics reveal specifics of how to build and sustain a highly successful European real estate business. Europe is a unique marketplace—from the overarching structure of the European Union to the diversity of countries that are located near one another but distinct. Add to that language differences, country-specific legal and tax structures, and cultural nuances, and conducting business in Europe is simply not the same as it is in the United States or Asia. Therefore, Europe presents leaders with specific challenges and opportunities that they can only address by embodying certain leadership traits and characteristics that are uniquely European.

This chapter revisits leadership discussions presented earlier in this book, but in the context of the three overarching themes, bringing together a portrait of the highly successful European real estate leader. Today's business and economic climate heightens the importance of understanding leadership. Even as economic recovery takes root across Europe, history indicates there will be future booms and busts. Cyclicity is the nature of the real estate business. If the industry as a whole is to have a chance of minimizing the impact of future downturns, it will be by heeding the wisdom of those who have weathered the last crisis—as well as the corrections and crashes that came before—through reliance on fundamental leadership qualities.

Following One's Instincts

The strong entrepreneurial streak among most European real estate leaders contradicts the conventional view of the broader class of European business leaders as conservative in nature, especially when compared with their stereotypically brash North American counterparts. The commonly held belief is that Europeans are more inclined to stay the course or follow the tried and true. Not so with European real estate leaders! In this sector, seasoned instincts are essential. European leaders, who have excelled in this difficult environment, will strike off on their own instead of merely following the crowd or playing it safe.

In changing and challenging times, the ability to identify emerging opportunity before everyone else drives success. Being an early mover carries risk, but also a substantial upside.

The instinctual leader is not wedded to one approach, but acknowledges the myriad forces of change, from economic cycles to demographic shifts that favor one city over another. This European leader also acknowledges that what has been viable in the past will be subject to evolution, such as the impact of e-commerce on retail real estate and the resulting greater importance of logistics and distribution centers.

Only by reexamining existing sectors and identifying new opportunities are entrepreneurial executives able to identify potential business concepts before the trend has been widely identified. "In the development business, there are so many different opportunities at any one time, so you really need to concentrate and focus on the right ones," says Otto of ECE Projektmanagement. Once opportunities are identified, such as recognizing emerging tenants with new concepts, it is up to the real estate leader to place the bet on the ones with the greatest potential.

Independent-mindedness allows leaders to pursue opportunities while staying ahead of the curve. But they must rally their organizations behind them. "Setting a path and energizing people are all part of leadership," says Salway of Land Securities.

It is not enough to scan the horizon for what is already happening; a leader anticipates the future and takes the risk before everyone else dives in. For example, in European real estate, early movers often invest soon after a downturn—the more challenging the downturn the better. "This is my third cycle," Orf of Apollo Global Management says of the current phase of downturn and recovery. "I think this one is the best from a buying-opportunity perspective."

To be a European real estate leader, one must be visionary and innovative. That means becoming comfortable with continuous change and seeking to be ahead of the trend while embracing reasonable exposure to risk. These are the attributes of the explorers/mapmakers. They do not follow the well-worn paths traveled by others, but instead seek to blaze their own trail, despite its complexity or a lack of visibility.

"The world is getting to be so complex and intertwined," says Zehner of LaSalle Investment Management. "Real estate leaders going forward will have to figure out what's happening to the euro, what's happening to weaker countries in the Eurozone, what's the level of economic growth, what's happening to the banks . . . "

These leaders follow their instincts, knowing that they will make mistakes, but with the knowledge that only by moving their boundaries can they discover new opportunities. And they need to act more quickly than in the past. "Activity is speeding up. The trends that in the past took five to ten years to play out are now playing out in 12 to 18 months," says Kavanagh of AXA Real Estate.

In contrast with their U.S. and other global counterparts, many European real estate leaders purposefully have lived, studied, and worked all over the world. They appreciate the cultural sensitivity required and the complexity of managing a global business.

An Appreciation for Culture and Complexity

Highly successful European real estate executives tend to have firsthand experience in different parts of the world, whether through their upbringing, education, or business ventures. This global view translates into a distinct advantage in building and managing a pan-European business. It stands in stark contrast with their American counterparts, most of whom lack sensitivity to the nuances of culture and complexity.

In the aftermath of the 2008–2009 global economic crisis, many European real estate firms retrenched, returning to their core markets. A firm that expanded beyond London, for example, might have returned there while reducing its holdings in other parts of Europe. Other organizations, however, have leaders whose personal and professional experiences have allowed them to succeed by integrating diverse cultural and social lessons into business decision making. "My whole life has been, one way or the other, influenced by diverse cultures, diverse languages, and diverse entities around the world," says Piani of Allianz Real Estate.

But because the risks are always unique, varying from place to place, models and strategies from one country cannot be imposed on another. "Absorb as much as you can from the environment, but every hypothesis that you are using has to be tested again and again," says Pereda of Grupo Lar.

An appreciation for culture and complexity encourages a leader to import knowledge from beyond his or her own borders, gaining the wisdom of lessons learned elsewhere—including lessons learned by others. Successful executives continuously expand their horizons through ongoing learning. Their appreciation for continual learning stems from their earliest experiences, often through formative interactions with mentors and role models. "I have been raised and educated with a certain ambition to get an international education. That was always part of my background," recalls Fautré of AG Real Estate.

Staying the Course: The Long-Term View

The third attribute most common among successful business leaders is staying true to a long-term view. Nowhere is this more evident than Europe—even though it may be considered counter to the entrepreneurial spirit present among European real estate leaders. Real estate is inherently a long-term proposition, yet the temptation is to fall victim to short-term thinking. The landscape is littered with the remains of those who came into European real estate late in the boom of 2005–2007, lured by the false promise of the quick profit. With no frame of reference for the cycles of the industry and believing that, as property values soared, the arrows would keep pointing upward, they overbought, overbuilt, and overleveraged. These short-term players were the first and most visible casualties of the downturn.

As Newsum recommends, "Keep an eye on those who really know what they are doing and ignore the short-term 'glamour players' who are trying to make money very fast. There is no need to make money so quickly."

The long-term view is important because most opportunities that emerge do not carry immediate payback. They require a vision, fortitude, and the right instincts. If this were not the case, these opportunities would already be on the radar of numerous competitors, making them much less attractive. Moreover, the long-term mind-set enables lessons learned from one region or experience to be applied to another. Even when unique local or regional variables are involved, a successful tactic or painful mistake informs subsequent decisions.

Taking a long-term view also reinforces a primary leadership goal— leaving a legacy. It is the ultimate destination of thoughtful leadership to leave a permanent mark for the benefit of others and society in general. In European real estate, legacy equates to stewardship. Distinguished leaders of companies with long histories take a thoughtful approach to development and revitalization. Even when commercial, industrial, or residential spaces need to be adapted to modern needs, the past is not forgotten. New and old can commingle in a way that honors both. The enduring nature of real estate assets also means that the actions one takes today will affect future generations. Stewardship and legacy, therefore, demand reflection before action is taken in order to consider the legacy one hopes to leave behind.

Legacy also means influencing the next generation—those who will follow in the footsteps of today's leaders. Those who are coming up the ranks will distinguish themselves as being truly wise if they learn from the experiences, positive and negative, of those who have come before them. Moreover, these leaders-in-the-making must be comfortable with the fact that taking risks in a business such as real estate does not automatically lead to reward.

"You have to make mistakes because mistakes are what create experience," observes Ritblat.

Lessons Learned

The leaders in European real estate profiled in this book offer a road map for the success of those who follow to continue the leadership journey. Unfortunately, there often tends to be high turnover among the newcomers—particularly among those who enter the business late in the boom cycle. They anticipate quick profits, which leads to excessive risk and leverage and exorbitant property prices. Many are washed out in the first wave of the downturn. As the leaders profiled in this book observe, the players who were burned last time are gone. For them, there is no hope of learning lessons to apply the next time because there is no next time. When the cycle overheats again, a new crop of speculators will enter, running the same risk of elimination by the same excesses.

That does not mean the lessons contained in this book are beyond the grasp of anyone else. The examples of today's leaders will prove valuable for anyone serious about participating in European real estate for the long term.

As philosopher and essayist George Santayana famously wrote, "Those who cannot remember the past are condemned to repeat it." The leadership lessons of the European real estate executives profiled in this book provide invaluable perspective on the past. For those who will follow, entering the business with no historical context of their own, the lessons learned here may very well solidify and preserve their careers.

It is a tall order, and many of those who enter the real estate market in Europe will fail to make the grade—a situation no different from that in any other part of the world. Those who avail themselves of the collective wisdom of the leaders who have come before them will have a distinct advantage. Managing a pan-European business, however, requires a unique skill set. Success is driven by having the courage to follow your instincts and yet invest with a long-term view.

Vision, patience, and a willingness to take risk, while taking the long-term view, are the keys to success, especially in real estate. Successful industry leaders who follow these principles will derive the intrinsic rewards from the hunt for opportunity and the satisfaction over time of seeing their investments and developments—literally—change the skyline.